Loon Magic

Loon Magic

Tom Klein

Preface by Sigurd T. Olson

Edited by Jeff Fair

PAPER BIRCH PRESS INC.

Ashland, WI

PHOTOS BY WOODY HAGGE

To the memory of Sigurd F. Olson (1899–1982)
who opened my mind and heart to the music of
the wilderness, and to his son, Sigurd T. Olson,
who helped me understand loons.

Second Edition, November, 1985

Paper Birch Press, Inc.
Box 128
Ashland, WI 54806

PHOTO BY WOODY HAGGE

ISBN 0-9613961-0-5
Library of Congress Card Number 84-062111

Acknowledgements

*L*oon Magic was not a solo effort. As detailed in *SOURCES*, many people shared their professional and personal experiences. A few deserve special recognition.

A full partner, Pat Klein provided research and editing support, production coordination and sound judgments which often sent the author trout fishing when *Loon Magic* approached the intensity of loon possession.

Jeff Fair was an excellent, insightful editor. His knowledge of both science and language are evident throughout the text.

The name Sigurd Olson appears frequently. The research of Sigurd T. Olson is, in fact, one of the pillars of the book. Another less visible but equally important pillar is the inspiration of Sig's father, Sigurd F. Olson, who died in January of 1982 after a half-century of conservation leadership.

My thanks to all the photographers who helped to bring loons to life, especially to Woody Hagge and Dr. Glenn Irwin, and to the fearless people who reviewed the draft manuscript—Wayne and Char Cordes, Dan Small, Mark Peterson, and Paul Hansen.

My thanks also to Kathy Mackey who found subtle errors missed by many less experienced proofreaders and to Arnell Lavasseur who demonstrated infinite patience while typing through seven revisions of the manuscript. And to Jim Pierce who gave me directions during my journeys through the scientific literature.

Finally special thanks to Grace and Charlie James who shared the serenity of "Stillwoods."

PHOTO BY MORGAN HEBARD

PHOTO BY TOM MANGELSEN

"The Lord did well when he put the loon and his music in the land."

—*Aldo Leopold*

It has been said that one's early childhood experiences are a basic force in molding what a person will be in later years. Loons have always been a part of my life. I can't remember when I first became aware of them but I have distinct childhood recollections of my parents stopping to watch or listen to a loon and hearing them say, "There's a loon!" or "Listen to the loons!" and always with a great sense of pleasure and excitement. No matter what the circumstances, paddling, portaging, picnicking or hiking, the presence of a loon always merited special notice and acknowledgement; and this from people who had no doubt seen thousands of loons over their years in the north!

I suppose that is why, in part at least, loons have become an indelible part of my being and why the lake country of Minnesota and Canada where I grew up is always synonymous with loons. This association is not privy only to me for I share it with almost everyone who has traveled and loved the lake country where common loons occur. While there is a certain degree of fascination inherent with all species of loons, it is the common loon which holds the greatest attraction and appeal for all. Its distinctive coloration, haunting wild calling, remarkable and often bizarre behavior patterns are all unique. No other species of loon exhibits these particular attributes or merits the status and attractiveness of the common loon in the minds of those who have come to know, love and respect this unusual north country denizen. These qualities occur, however, primarily on its northern summer ranges. On its wintering grounds its appeal to observers is greatly reduced or lost as the loons assume their winter plumage and a much more retiring comportment and demeanor.

To me, it is most significant that almost without exception, loons, wildness and wilderness are always considered concurrently. Although loons are at their best in true wilderness situations, they also occur in non-wilderness areas. However, in the minds of those who encounter loons, no matter where, the images, impressions and feelings of true wilderness automatically surface and strongly assert themselves. The loon's freedom, independence, and simplicity characterize the true spirit of wilderness. Its wild, weird calling does more to create the indescribable feeling of being apart from civilization and being close to the primitive than any other natural phenomenon in the wilderness country.

The ancient impulses, urges, fears and wonder are much closer to the surface than most realize. In fact, an interesting paradox sometimes exists. While most people react positively and thrill to these primal feelings inspired by the sight and sounds of loons, some experience actual dread and fear. Of primary importance, however, is the close instinctive association with wilderness and its values, which characterizes in the truest sense the very spirit of wildness, freedom, independence, simplicity, mystery and exultation. Dr. Walter J. Breckenridge was most eloquent when he described his feelings: " . . . to me it expresses the essence of unrestrained wildness and seems to put the stamp of gen-

uineness on a North Country setting like 'Sterling' does on silver . . . ''

The wild calling of loons does more for me to create the sense of being apart from civilization and again being close to the primitive than almost any other phenomenon except perhaps for the howling of wolves. If the presence and calling of loons creates only these feelings for those who see and hear them it would be important enough; however, they also undeniably verify that wilderness is an actuality, and they punctuate it graphically with their presence.

For travelers and residents of the northern lake country, the frequent occurrence of loons creates a ready source of highly valued enjoyment. Unlike most wildlife, they are seldom wary or secretive. They are readily observed as they go about their daily routines, save perhaps for their nesting activities. It is not uncommon to see loons many times during the course of a day's paddle. Listening to the spectacular spectrum of calls and observing their wild, unpredictable behavior provides a true wilderness viewing opportunity rarely experienced with other species of wildlife.

Because loons are unquestionably an integral part of the wilderness idea, any knowledge that can be developed to shed more light on the management of wilderness lands and loons is vital to their continued well-being. To this end, in 1950 I spent one of the most interesting and challenging years of my young life gathering basic data on the status and natural history of loons for a thesis. At that time, information concerning loons was scant and fragmentary at best, and almost everything I discovered was new and exciting. Since then much more has been done and increasingly sophisticated and comprehensive studies and investigations are underway over most of the loon ranges in North America. They are now providing critical information needed to better understand the loon's ecological niche.

Public awareness and appreciation of loons has become a full-blown love affair, increasing far beyond any early expectations, and has expressed itself in some unusual though perhaps predictable ways. The common loon has now become the official state bird for Minnesota; it is eagerly sought after as a subject for hosts of artists and photographers, and salable items featuring loons ranging from elegant silver jewelry to tee-shirts can be found in nearly every gift and specialty shop in the north country. The importance of the loon in this day and age can scarcely be denied.

Those who know the lake country of the north, as well as those who are only occasional visitors, have embraced the loon not only as an authentic symbol of wilderness, but as a vital component of wilderness itself. And now, we will have at our disposal a definitely delightful, infinitely usable, state-of-the art publication documenting the life and times of the common loon as we know it today. The loon has definitely come of age!

Sigurd T. Olson
Douglas, Alaska
December 10, 1984

PHOTO BY TOM MANGELSEN

*"No one who has ever heard the diver's music—
the mournful far-carrying callnotes and the
uninhibited, cacophonous, crazy laughter—
can ever forget it."*

—*Oliver Austin, 1961*

At a 1984 Minnesota wildlife conference, Ruth Norris, Senior Editor of *Audubon* magazine, estimated the United State's "birder" population at about thirty million. In the *Audubon Society Encyclopedia of North American Birds*, the editor estimated the U.S. summer population of birds at about six billion. While 200 birds for every birder doesn't seem like a bad ratio, bird people are known to be very particular. In fact, many can't stand the sight of crows or starlings and consider robins or wrens passé. Most birders have a preferred family: there are thrush people, swallow people, heron people, falcon people, crane people and probably a few phalarope people. And then there are loon people. Perhaps the most irrational of birders, loon people often confine their avian interest to just a single species—*Gavia immer*, the common loon.

Their attraction to this bird is decidedly abnormal. I know many otherwise intelligent and sensible people who surround themselves with loon "trinkets", give money to various loon causes and speak of little else but loons in the

PHOTO BY TOM MANGELSEN

privacy of their lakeshore cabins. And a few try, like Katharine Hepburn in *On Golden Pond,* to talk to loons. Maybe some even succeed.

It is evident that a "loon religion" is evolving in many northern lake communities. The annual Loon Festival on the shores of Lake Winnipesaukee in New Hampshire is a sign of the times, as is the popularity of the *Voices of the Loon* record album. In Mercer, Wisconsin the faithful have even constructed a nineteen foot "idol" of their favorite bird. Over the past few years, the loon has become the symbol for the northern experience—a mystique which draws thousands of urban refugees from the concrete caverns of New York, Detroit, Chicago, Milwaukee and Minneapolis, north to Loon Country.

This is a book for loon people. Not an ornithological textbook, it is intended to be an accurate and interesting look at loons. The product of careful research and review by many technical experts, *Loon Magic* explains scientific terms and concepts without using other scientific terms and concepts.

It is meant to be read, not studied. No scientific axes grinding, *Loon Magic* presents the loon with no preconceived notions or rules. The book's theme is simple: loons are just loons; they do not mirror the minds or values of their lakeshore admirers.

While *Loon Magic* contains information about all four species of loons, by design and circumstance it focuses upon the common loon. By design, because the common loon is the only loon of the contiguous states and southern Canada, and because it is the glamour bird (Sorry, eagles!) of northern lakes. And by circumstance, because so little is known about the "other three": the arctic, yellow-billed and red-throated loons.

While the research phase of *Loon Magic* involved tracking down every scientific article, thesis, essay, field guide, monograph and rumor connected with loons, this library work was a small part of the effort. Far more important

PHOTOS BY LYNN ROGERS

were the discussions with dozens of field scientists and amateur loon watchers. The acceptance of information from non-scientists will, no doubt, be viewed with horror by some. So be it. I'll take the word anyday of a lakeside resident who has seriously observed loons for twenty or thirty years over the opinion of a pressured graduate student whose commitment to loons usually encompasses only one or two summers.

But the most important ingredient in *Loon Magic,* the animating influence, was my own loon watching. Not studying loons . . . I'm not a scientist. Just watching. And enjoying. Ever since my first trip in the Minnesota-Ontario canoe country, loons have been, at least mentally, a constant companion. For me, loons have been important. For me, loon music is more than a pleasant distraction while fishing or paddling; it is often the prelude to a powerful spiritual experience.

Many people clearly recall their first experience with loons and people almost always remember the first time they heard loon music. I'm slightly embarrassed to admit I don't. While boyhood trips to northern Wisconsin produced a few loon encounters, nothing special happened. It wasn't until August of 1965 on the Minnesota-Canada border that loons grabbed my soul. With Bill Richtsmeier, a high school buddy, I drove to Moose Lake, a little ways north of Ely, to start a great Boundary Waters adventure.

We brought everything on that trip, including a six pound tackle box, an axe, two machetes, two sleeping bags worthy of an arctic expedition, and a steel ammo case to protect our eight pounds of bacon. After a long day's paddle and portage, we made it to Louisa Falls at the bottom of Agnes Lake, just over the Canadian border. Shoulders bright red from the August sun and sore from the sharp bite of the thin Duluth-pack straps, we settled into the campsite surrounded by a reassuring audio backdrop of falling water.

The loons on Agnes called that night, probably no louder nor more often than they do on any other August night. But the calling found the right spot. We sat by the campfire bewitched, anticipating two weeks of granite cliffs, water diamonds on the shimmering lakes, firm lake trout, spongy sphagnum moss and quiet evenings with the voices of the wilderness.

That night on Agnes we didn't know the difference between the tremolo, wail or yodel. And we didn't care. We just soaked it all in. It was a magical night. I haven't kept track of Bill over the passing years so I can't speak for him, but nothing has been the same for me since.

PHOTO BY TOM KLEIN

Contents

Looking for Loons

Loon People

*"A beautiful sight was that of three loons facing the rising sun, standing almost erect
on the water, their great wings vigorously flapping, the sun shining full upon their
pure white breasts. It seemed almost like an act of religious devotion in honor of old
Phoebus."*

—Rev. M. B. Townsend, 1919

Loons are part of many people's religion. Julius Dinger, a real estate appraiser, summers at Hurd Lake, just north of his Eau Claire, Wisconsin home. That's where he got to know loons and where loons got to him. An admitted loon fanatic, Julius, when he dies, doesn't want hymns played. He wants a special service: "I suppose this will sound a little silly to most people, but when I pass away, the music I want at my memorial service is the call of the loon," says Dinger. Loon magic at work.

Ken and Chip Sorlien live on Squam Lake, the real golden pond, in New Hampshire's rugged lake country. A retired General Mills sales executive, Ken moved north from Boston just to watch the peaceful waters of Squam, but he watches much more now. As a volunteer coordinator for the elaborate loon protection effort on the lake, he spends thirty to forty hours a week watching Squam's loons and keeping track of the other volunteers. In 1984, his efforts paid a personal dividend when a loon pair nesting on an artificial nest island right in front of his home turned an egg into a chick. Ken and Chip offered a 7:30 a.m. champagne toast from their pier. More loon magic.

Grace James lives with her husband, Charlie, in Milwaukee, but her soul is to be found on Stone Lake, a small but attractive northern Wisconsin lake. Grace has four children, but every summer her family expands by three or four members. The Stone Lake loons, you see, are hers. She watches them, talks to them and protects them. When an unsuspecting fisherman strays a little too close to the island where her loons always nest, Grace grabs the bullhorn she keeps handy and shouts across the lake: "Keep away, don't you know loons are on that island?" It always works. Later she rows out and explains to the fisherman the special considerations nesting loons deserve. Once, when a red-tailed hawk swooped over an adult loon with two chicks, Grace raced out of her cabin frantically waving a towel to frighten away the potential predator. For her antics she has picked up the nickname "Loony Grace," but she doesn't mind. She lives in a world of loon magic.

PHOTO BY TOM MANGELSEN

...oklet on loons, *North to Open Water*, Grace James started the "loon ... in Wisconsin.   PHOTO BY TOM KLEIN

... is a *loon ranger* on Squam Lake for The New Hampshire Loon Pres-
...ommittee.   PHOTO BY TOM KLEIN

These people have lots of company; the loon's spell has spread across the Northeast and Midwest. In Wisconsin, over seven hundred people volunteer to monitor the loon populations on their lakes. In New Hampshire, nearly 3,000 people make contributions of time and money to the Loon Preservation Committee. In Michigan, volunteers of the Whitefish Point Bird Observatory are on Lake Superior's shore at dawn on chilling April and May mornings to count migrating loons.

Why? What is so enchanting about a stout black and white bird that likes to call when most people like to sleep? Part of the answer might be the distance loons and people have traveled together. In the 1983 film *A Quest For Fire*, set in the dawn of human origins, loon calls were used extensively in the sound track. It was a forgettable film but it had one memorable scene depicting a band of primitive humans stopping to listen to that call so familiar yet so haunting. No one knows if a half a million years ago the loon's call was the same sound that echoed last summer around Squam in New Hampshire or Saganaga in Minnesota. But it could have been.

If the call of the loon does go back to our first days as humans, the strong feelings of *déjà vu* many people experience when hearing loon calls would be more understandable and the pull of loon magic a bit less mysterious. Sigurd F. Olson often wrote about *racial memory*, the ability of a person to recall, however vaguely, the common thoughts, feelings or experiences of ancestors from thousands of years ago. The romantic poets of the nineteenth century understood the concept. So do people who accept the concept of reincarnation.

Like the call of the loon, the howl of the wolf has this power to take people back. In an article on wolves for *Smithsonian* magazine, novelist David Nevin detailed his profound response to a wolf howl: the recognition " . . . went far back, it flowed from that pool of inherited knowledge we all carry from the past. I'd have known it anywhere."

Cynics will attribute such insights to harmless fantasy or delusion; empirically-minded scientists might, with a condescending nod, toss the idea of racial memory into a class of phenomena which can neither be proved nor disproved.

Loons in Native American Culture

But the idea intrigues Keewaydinoquay, an Ojibwa who teaches ethnobiology at the University of Wisconsin-Milwaukee. Kee (she prefers her Ojibwa name) recalls that loons were an important part of her childhood on Beaver Island, a small island in Lake Michigan off the northeastern shore of Wisconsin. She would communicate with loons by offering *kaneck,* a blend of sacred herbs, which she placed on the shore. Loons would come to share and accept her offering. A bond was formed.

Over a lengthy breakfast interview, Kee told me a powerful story, *Brave is Mahng is Loon,* about the origins of the Ojibwa. In the story the loon was not just another bird, but the first act of creation when the very voice of the Creator echoed across the void and became embodied in a gray and black shadow, the spirit of the loon. Later, Sun threw light on the shadow, giving Loon his striking white markings. Loon loved Anishinabe, the first man. It was Loon who saved Anishinabe when, while swimming, his long black hair became entangled in logs.

And so the magic began a long time ago. It's easy to imagine how Kee's story developed: a bright campfire reflected in the eyes of an ancient people alive with creativity and wonder, a people curious about their origins and their relationship to the natural world. A vibrant tremolo call halted the conversation, moved it in new directions . . . .

The legend reflects the special relationship between loons and the Ojibwa. In the Ojibwa language, *mahng* is the word for both brave and loon. In the "Song of Hiawatha," Longfellow praised Hiawatha with a reference to loons:

From the red deer's flesh Nokomis
Made a banquet to his honor.
All the village came and feasted,
All the guests praised Hiawatha,
Called him Strong-Heart, *Soan-ge-taha!*
Called him Loon-Heart, *Mahn-go-taysee!*

Mahn-go-taysee, translated by Kee as "thou art a loon-hearted one," is about the finest compliment an Ojibwa can pay another person.

The very first accounts of the chemistry between loons and people were not written by Longfellow, nor told by Native American storytellers; they can be seen only on the granite outcroppings of the Canadian Shield, north of the Great Lakes. Crude pictographs of loons still grace some of those rock faces. Even after hundreds or thousands of years, these red images, made with hematite and fish oil, cling to the rocks. Little is known of their origins; no oral traditions interpret them or offer a clue to the identity or motives of their makers.

Anthropologists know only that some people lived in the region about 8,000 years ago, following the edge of the great ice sheets. Later, about 5,000 years ago, a group known as the Old Copper Culture people inhabited the Upper Great Lakes and left copper mines and tools as testimony of their presence. Native Americans, defined only as the Early Woodland Culture, used the area until about the birth of Christ and left burial mounds, pottery and pipes. Then we start getting into "recorded history." The first Europeans entered the north country in the early 1600s. Any of these groups or none of them could have painted loons on granite cliffs. We just don't know. But with eloquent silence, these paintings remind us simply that moose, canoes, abstract deities and loons were part of the lives of a mysterious people.

Far more is known of the Ojibwa people who moved into the Upper Great Lakes region in the early seventeenth century. The Ojibwa, like most Native American tribes, structured their society through a system of clans. The clan was patrilineal: your father's clan became your clan. According to Delores Bainbridge, an Ojibwa storyteller living in Ashland, Wisconsin, the five great clans of her tribe—the Loon, Crane, Bear, Martin and Fish clans—came out of the waters at the mouth of the St. Lawrence River.

According to William Warner, author of *A History of the Ojibway Nation*, the head of the Loon Clan was known for wisdom, honesty and bravery. In her comprehensive study of Ojibwa music, Frances Densmore uncovered songs of the loon which were sung by warriors preparing for battle. If a loon were heard calling on the eve of the warpath, it was considered an omen of victory.

Loon legends span the continent. While some are obscure like the story from eastern Canada of Tatler, a loon who served as the eyes and ears of The Creator, Gloosaph, others like the Tsimshian Indian legend of the loon's necklace are well known. Stories of a loon woman are known in several Indian cultures. The Cree of northern Canada believed the loon's call was the cry of slain warriors calling back to the land of the living.

In the Pacific Northwest, a legend from the east side of the Olympic Peninsula related the story of an Indian boy who disobeyed his mother by swimming in a lake inhabited by evil spirits who turned the boy into a loon. The boy returned to his home but could speak only in the harsh cries of a loon and was chased away by his mother, an obvious lesson on the dangers of disobedience. Many Indian loon legends have similar practical objectives.

Probably no native peoples have more references to loons in their folklore than the Eskimo. *Tuutlick*, the most frequent Eskimo name for the common loon, turns up in dozens of Eskimo legends, including the Bering Strait Eskimo story of Soolook, a boy blinded by his evil witchdoctor mother. One day Soolook followed the call of a loon to a small lake where the loon restored his sight. Thanking the loon, Soolook spoke for generations of Eskimos when he said, "The spirit of one's good friend, the loon, shall always be the favorite spirit of one's children and their children's children." The existence of over thirty different Eskimo names for the four species of loons speaks to the importance of loons for the Eskimo. Well into the twentieth century, loons were part of the culture and commerce of the Eskimo. For the Nunamiut Eskimos, the loon had a variety of uses. It was used for food and valued as a source of fat; the bill of the yellow-billed loon was used for headband decorations and the skin of the neck, which is very tough, was used to make boots and parkas.

In 1910, Bernhard Hantzsch traveled to Baffin Island where he observed substantial numbers of common and arctic loons and a few red-throated loons. His journal, however, details the extensive robbing of loon nests by Eskimos, which resulted in the collapse of local loon populations. Hantzsch offered an editorial note on the practice: "But as such recklessness is natural to primitive man, and as restriction of hunting through game laws is out of the question here, Nature herself must see to the management of her highest creation." For other Eskimos, though, the loon was sacred. One group in Northwest Alaska upheld a strict taboo against the killing of any loons.

Many Eskimo tribes venerated the loon in their art. Most museum collections of Eskimo art contain loon images. The Bering Sea Eskimos devised elaborate loon masks and carved loon decoys for use as fish net floats. Excavations of prehistoric Eskimo villages near Point Hope, Alaska uncovered loon heads carved out of walrus ivory.

The pervasive occurrence of the loon in the art and oral traditions of Native Americans across the North American continent is vivid testimony to the magnetism of this bird of the north and to the roots of the loon magic which still grips northern people.

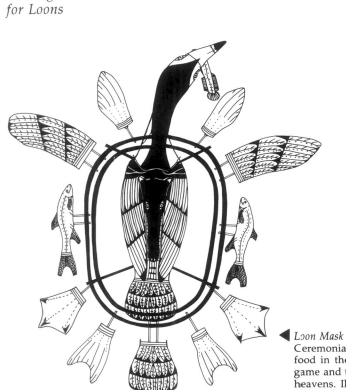

◀ *Loon Mask*
Ceremonial masks similar to this one were used centuries ago by Eskimos. The food in the loon's mouth may have symbolized a hunter's wish for abundant game and the concentric hoops and grooves may have represented the stars and heavens. Illustration based upon museum artifact at the Alaska State Museum, Juneau.

▶ *The Loon Tree*
A loon totem pole from Southeast Alaska. Illustration based upon photograph in *The Wolf and the Raven: Totem Poles of Southeast Alaska.*

◀ *Fishing Float*
Fishing floats shaped like loons were used by Eskimos to buoy the end of gill nets which were set at right angles from the shore. Illustration based upon museum artifact at the Alaska State Museum, Juneau.

ILLUSTRATIONS BY ERICA PETERSON

New Legends Unfold

Like staring into a campfire or watching a river flow, listening to loons has a hypnotic effect which transcends time. It has a power at the edge of rationality. Fifty years ago a woman spent just one summer on Lake Winnipesaukee in New Hampshire where the loons worked their spell. Last year she made a financial contribution to the Loon Preservation Committee, commenting that she remembered the "wonderful calling at night" and just wanted to help. Nearly 10,000 others have expressed similar feelings by contributing to private loon organizations in six states and one province. Something is going on here.

In the early twentieth century Charlton Ogburn, Jr. wrote *The Meaning of Birds,* an intriguing essay. No mystic or spiritualist by any means, Ogburn nevertheless found just the right words to describe the power of birds: "Birds are translators for us, the intermediaries between the vast world beyond us and our own emotions, expressing in their notes, in tones within our spiritual register, the nature of our common setting . . . " Amen.

As translators, loons are multi-lingual: they spoke to the early Cree, Ojibwa and Inuit and they speak to people today. Loons spoke very clearly to Joe Anderlik. A retired paper company executive living in Arlington Heights, a Chicago suburb, Anderlik heard the loon's call as a boy. He even remembers the year—1929. It was a sound he would never forget, a sound which would draw him back to the north country many times. Now, instead of stolen days up north, Anderlik spends every summer at his lake home near Lac du Flambeau in northern Wisconsin. He begins his daily routine at four in the morning when he goes to his workbench and starts carving, you guessed it, loons. He loves every minute of his work and his carvings show it. Joe has found his niche in loon country.

Having watched many people fall for loons, he sees a definite pattern: "People come up north from the city and hear this strange bird. This creates a lodestone. They carry the memories, often for years. Eventually they start spending more and more time up north. Pretty soon, they're living up here. Once they fall in love with loons, it's forever." Joe understands loons. He has touched the magic.

There are thousands of people like Joe scattered around the northland. It's difficult to separate their love for loons and their love for the place loons happen to be. It could be that loons reinforce for people their image of the north country. The similarity of some of the northern lakes of Maine and Minnesota or of New Hampshire and Wisconsin is remarkable; all loon country exudes that rugged northern beauty. But maybe the question is moot, loons and loon country being one, symbol and substance, player and stage— a captivating creature in a magical land.

Joe Anderlik of Arlington Heights, Illinois doing what comes naturally—carving loons.   PHOTO BY MIKE SEELING

Family Album

"The study of birds is to me like the study of man. It demands more than one faculty, and the end is not so much the elucidation of great laws, such as we may expect to derive from examination of the physical universe, as the delineation of character."
—*Charlton Ogburn, Jr., 1915*

The Classification of Birds

Phylum . . . superclass . . . subspecies . . . genus . . . suborder . . . superfamily . . . subclass . . . order . . . kingdom . . . . The classification of birds is a playground for ornithologists. If your primary interest is loons, however, you're in luck. Nearly every bird book begins with loons, the oldest living birds. Their classification is simple with no suborders, superclasses or even subspecies to clutter their listing.

Taxonomists, scientists specializing in the classification of plants and animals, use only eight categorical levels to sort out the common loon:

Kingdom:	*Animalia*—all animals including man
Phylum:	*Chordata*—animals with spinal cord
Subphylum:	*Vertebrata*—animals with solid backbone
Class:	*Aves*—all birds
Order:	*Gaviiformes*—the loon group
Family:	*Gaviidae*—the only family of loons
Genus:	*Gavia*—the group of four loon species
Species:	*immer*—one of four loon species

The scientific name for any bird simply combines the genus and species names. For example, *Gavia immer* is the common loon, which is one of four distinct species of the family *Gaviidae*. The loon's family tree is bare: unlike most orders of birds, the order *Gaviiformes* has only one family, the *Gaviidae*. If your passion were small perching birds, you would encounter the order *Passeriformes*, holding no less than twenty-nine families including the thrush family with 306 species and the finch family with 436 species. With loons, it's one family and only four species.

The classification system is a straight-forward method of keeping birds organized. It provides sharp, if somewhat arbitrary, boundaries for the complex and often confusing natural order by establishing a clear hierarchy from the general to the specific. The bird classification system works somewhat like the United States election system, with birds and voters organized at many levels. While the most general level for voters is the nation and for birds the class, voters are then divided by states and birds by orders. (The names of all bird orders end with the suffix "*-iformes.*") Beyond the state level, voters are organized by counties and birds by families. Counties have a smaller unit, the city, and bird families have a more specific grouping, the genus. Finally, voters are classed within the city by precinct and birds are classed within the genus by species, the most specific level of classification.

What's in a Name?

The generic name for loons is *Gavia*, from which order and family names are derived. Old bird books used *Gavia* for both loons and sea smews, a Eurasian merganser which only rarely wanders onto the North American continent. Since smews resemble loons in neither appearance nor habit, it is odd that loons carry *Gavia* as half of their scientific name. Loon fanciers can take some pleasure, though, in the sure knowledge that loons are far more famous than smews.

The species name *immer* is Scandinavian. Its root, the Swedish word *emmer*, meaning the blackened ashes of fire, is a fitting reference to the common loon's contrasting black and white plumage. *Immer* is also the contemporary Norwegian word for loon. Several researchers, though, point to the Latin *immerus*, meaning submerged, as another possible source for *immer*.

The common loon has not always had *Gavia immer* as its scientific name. The ten-volume *Century Dictionary*, edited by William Dwight Whitney in 1899, contains a description of the common loon with two scientific names, *Colymbus torquatusor* and *Colymbus glacialis.* Although it refers to ice, the second option has a pleasant warmth. For years, scientists kept changing their minds about the proper place for loons in the bird world. The 1917 edition of *Birds of America* edited by Gilbert Pearson placed loons in the order *Pygopodes* with the company of auks and grebes. The name game ended in 1950 when the International Commission of Zoological Nomenclature gave the common loon

its current, and presumably final, scientific name.

The bird's popular or common name "loon" has been around a long time. Most bird books list two possible sources: the English word *lumme*, meaning lummox or awkward person, and the old Scandinavian word *lom*, meaning lame or clumsy. In both cases the point is clear. As any veteran loon watcher knows, loons can be ridiculously clumsy and almost helpless on land. The *Century Dictionary*, however, has a different etymological approach. Its editor believed loon to be a corruption of the Provincial English word *loom*, meaning the "track of a fish", which probably described the wake a fish makes while swimming just under the surface.

Of the four species of loons, the three of the far north—the arctic, yellow-billed and red-throated loons—carry proud,

The sturdy beak, smooth head and dramatic red eye are characteristics of the common loon. PHOTO BY WOODY HAGGE

descriptive names. But is the other loon really "common"? To most, it's a spectacular bird. The name may be unfair, but the common loon is in the good company of the common egret, the common merganser, and the common sandpiper. With all the truly great bird names like royal tern, great egret, golden-crowned kinglet or magnificent frigate bird, there should have been one more exciting name to help out the common loon. Considering there are least bitterns, lesser goldfinches, and even parasitic jaegers, it could have been worse. Perhaps the number of "other" names for the common loon have been a response to this injustice. The common loon has flown under such interesting names as the great northern diver, the ring-necked loon, the black-billed loon, the ember goose and the walloon. By any name, the common loon is a special bird.

How Old is Old

Loons are the first birds on the American Ornithologists Union's (AOU) *Check-list of North American Birds,* and by no coincidence. The check-list is a phylogenetic ranking, a listing of birds from the lowest, most primitive orders, to the highest, most recently evolved orders. While L. L. Snyder, Curator of Ornithology for the Royal Ontario Museum of Zoology, calls loons an "old and distinguished group of birds which have changed very little," the exact age of the loon species is open to speculation.

A bit of bird history is required to help place the loon in perspective. The first known player on the avian stage was *archaeopteryx,* dating back about 140 million years. Fifty million years later, about the time *Tyrannosaurus rex* dominated the landscape, the genus *Hesperornis* entered the scene. In 1870, Professor March of Yale University found fragments of this ancient bird in western Kansas. Drawn from fossil remains, artist's renderings of *Hesperornis* look remarkably like present day loons, but *Hesperornis* was about six-feet tall and probably flightless. While scientists contend *Hesperornis* was not a direct loon ancestor, the editors of *The Audubon Society Encyclopedia of North American Birds* do note that it was "in form and habit much like a loon of today." So loon-like birds go back about ninety million years.

A much smaller bird, and certainly a loon relative, has been described by Robert Storer. Writing in the bird journal *Auk,* Storer postulates that loons separated from primitive gull-like stock between the late *Cretaceous* period and early *Eocene* epoch, roughly fifty to eighty million years ago. While no fossils of loons from that era have been discovered, a loon fossil *Columboides minutes* was studied by Storer. Found in France, this twenty million year old bird was only ten to twelve inches in length and, according to Storer, probably flew more frequently than today's loons. Not all birds have such ancient lineage. The larks came along less than ten million years ago and tanagers are real newcomers, having

Loons ride low in the water and always seem to be alert.
PHOTO BY WOODY HAGGE

appeared just ten thousand years ago.

Loons and Grebes

Early ornithologists believed the loon to be closely related to the grebe. Classed as a family of twenty worldwide species (including six in North America) within the order *Podicipediformes,* grebes share many traits with loons. Flying with legs straight out and neck hunched down, grebes have a similar profile. And like loons they are waterbirds with well-developed diving abilities. Grebes also demonstrate a few behaviors typical of loons, such as shared nest building and incubation, backriding of chicks and the running start before flight. Despite these many similarities, however, grebes are very different birds. Much smaller in size, grebes have partially webbed lobed toes, while loons have fully-webbed feet. Grebes are quick divers, but reach depths of only twenty feet, compared to a loon's dive of over 100 feet. There are also many physiological differences such as the number of neck vertebrae and arrangement of plumage which differentiate the two groups. Loons and grebes may share some lakes, but they do not share the same branch of the family tree.

The Four Species of Loons

If a population of birds or animals becomes geographically isolated by glaciation, mountain formation or other large-scale natural processes, an opportunity for speciation is created. Small changes in distinct geographical groups can lead, over thousands of years, to the development of a new species. Loons have had plenty of time (millions of years) and plenty of room (most of North America) to allow for the development of isolated populations. Why four species of loons emerged instead of two or twenty is academic. We do know that of about 8,000 species of birds, four are loons—the common, arctic, red-throated and yellow-billed. Or do we?

Sverre Sjolander and Greta Agren, two biologists from the University of Stockholm, aren't so sure. While studying both common and yellow-billed loons, they observed no "major differences between *Gavia immer* [common] and *Gavia adamsii* [yellow-billed] in reproductive and territorial behavior." They left open the possibility that *Gavia adamsii* is, in fact, a subspecies of *Gavia immer.* L. L. Snyder does not accept that view. In his book *Arctic Birds of Canada,* Snyder noted the differences in bill shape and necklace pattern, as well as size, adding that there are "no field observations which indicate these forms [common and yellow-billed] interbreed, even though the overlapping ranges in northwest Canada provide opportunities to mingle." Since relatively few studies of the yellow-billed loon have been undertaken, more research is needed before the common and yellow-billed question is finally settled.

There has been discussion regarding subspecies of the common loon for many years. Bird books as late as Frank Chapman's 1939 *Handbook of Birds in Eastern North America* list a common loon subspecies, *Gavia immer elasson* (the "lesser loon"), defined by a smaller size alone. While there is considerable geographical size variation for the common loon, the scientific community now recognizes only one common loon, *Gavia immer.* Many bird books and museum collections have also divided the arctic loon into subspecies, usually the Pacific arctic and green-throated arctic. While slight variations of size and plumage may occur, there is no acceptance by scientists today for more than one arctic loon, *Gavia arctica.*

A Family Portrait
Arctic loon, *Gavia arctica*

All loons are attractive, but the arctic loon is stunning. Its breeding plumage has a common loon's checkerboard back, but an arctic's neck has diagonal white stripes and the head is a regal silver gray. The bill of the arctic is smaller

The arctic loon in breeding plumage is a photographer's dream.
PHOTO BY GARY JONES

The red-throated loon is the smallest loon.
PHOTO BY STEPHEN KRASEMANN/DRK PHOTO

The yellow-billed loon is the largest of the loon family. Note the substantial nest.
PHOTO BY EDGAR JONES

The common loon is found throughout Canada and the northern tier of states.
PHOTO BY WOODY HAGGE

than a common's and is perfectly straight. Although its winter plumage is similar to that of the common, the arctic loon shows a stronger contrast between the dark upperparts and light underparts.

Overall, the arctic is a small loon with a length of twenty-three to twenty-nine inches, wingspread of forty-three to fifty inches, and weight of four to five pounds, compared to the common loon's length of twenty-eight to thirty-six inches, wingspread of fifty to fifty-eight inches and weight of seven to nine pounds.

In North America the arctic loon breeds from Alaska to the southern end of Hudson Bay and north to Baffin and Banks Islands. According to Ira Gabrielson and Frederick Lincoln, authors of *Birds of Alaska*, this breeding range includes central and northern British Columbia, northern Saskatchewan and northern Manitoba. The arctic loon winters along the Pacific Coast from Alaska down to southern California and Baja California. Only rarely have arctic loons been reported off the Atlantic coast. On the other side of the world, arctic loons are known to breed in Scotland, northern Scandinavia and Siberian Russia, and to winter off the coasts of Japan and Korea.

Preferring deep freshwater lakes for breeding, its distribution overlaps that of the red-throated, yellow-billed and, less frequently, the common loon. Like the common loon, the arctic loon lays one or two eggs and incubates them for twenty-eight to thirty days. Also like the common loon, the arctic uses a wide range of nest surfaces varying from bare ground to fairly large mounds of earth and vegetation and prefers islands and sheltered bays as nesting sites.

Except for its alarm call, which is very similar to a common's tremolo, the vocalizations of the arctic loon are unique. They are usually described as guttural with a wide range of wails, shrieks, squeals and yelps. After listening to arctic loons for several months in Alaska, one researcher compared their call to the bark of a dog, while another compares the call to the cackle of a hen. When disturbed, the arctic loons can emit a high pitched squeal. According to Gabrielson and Lincoln, arctic loons on their breeding grounds are "among the noisiest of all waterfowl." They quote one naturalist who found the wail heart-breaking and added, "if ever a species enjoyed spreading sorrow through the bird world it is this loon." Looking at the dramatic breeding plumage of the arctic loon, it is difficult to relate such beauty with sorrow. Probably to other arctic loons the vocalizations are sweet music—it's all in the ear of the listener.

Red-throated loon, *Gavia stellata*

The red-throated loon is the most widely distributed loon, ranging throughout northern Eurasia and in the tundra areas of northern North America from Alaska to Quebec, including the maritime areas of northeast Canada and Newfoundland. It breeds as far south as northern British Columbia. In the late 40s and 50s, it was reported to nest on the north shore of Lake Superior but none are found there today. In Alaska and the Canadian arctic regions, the red-throated is the most numerous of the loon species. In *Birds of Alaska*, the red-throated loon is described as breeding on "any suitable habitat found in Alaska." It winters on both the Pacific and Atlantic Coasts and occasionally on the Great Lakes, particularly Lake Michigan. In Europe, the red-throated loon winters over a wide area including the British Isles, the Mediterranean, Black and Caspian Seas and off the coast of Japan.

The smallest of the family members, the red-throated loon weighs about four pounds and is often described as being shy. It has a slender, slightly upturned bill. In breeding plumage the bright red throat makes it easy to identify, and it is the only loon without a black-and-white breeding plumage. In winter plumage, the red-throated loon is paler than the other loons. In many ways, it is an altogether different loon. The Royal Ontario Museum's L. L. Snyder suggests that the red-throated loon differs more from other loons than the other loons differ amongst themselves. He claims it is the "least 'loonish' of the loons."

Partly because of its smaller size, the red-throated loon can take flight from water with a very short running start. Naturalist Edward Howe Forbush commented that the red-throated loon can " . . . rise readily and fly from even a small pool, springing into the air with little difficulty." This mobility opens up smaller lakes and ponds for nesting and feeding, providing some isolation from the three other loon species. Where the range of red-throated and arctic loons overlap, the red-throated will usually be found on smaller ponds than the larger, and more aggressive arctic loon.

While the diet of the red-throated loon is primarily

A nesting red-throated loon caught turning eggs with its beak.
PHOTO BY STEPHEN KRASEMANN/DRK PHOTO

fish, it will, like the other loon species, occasionally feed on leeches, snails and aquatic insects. On salt water, the red-throated loon feeds on sculpins (a small bottom-dwelling fish), capelin, codfish and gunnel. While the red-throated is an excellent diver, it does not dive as deeply as the common loon.

Robert Bergman and Dirk Derksen studied red-throated loons off Storbersen Point in northern Alaska, an area where both red-throated and arctic loons nest. The researchers found that the two species did not socialize. While the arctic loons spent most of their time on the larger freshwater ponds, the red-throated loons flew to the coasts where the arctic cod provided table fare. They watched red-throated loons make repeated trips from nest sites on freshwater ponds to the Beaufort Sea carrying fish crosswise in their bills. Bergman and Derksen also noted that the red-throated loons preferred island nest sites, selecting islands eighty-eight percent of the time. The nest sites were often used for more than one year. Of twenty-seven nest sites, nineteen were used in consecutive years. The researchers found that nesting success for red-throated loons was much greater for the traditional sites than for first-time sites.

A team from the University of North Dakota studying yellow-billed loons just west of Prudhoe Bay in northern Alaska had occasion to watch red-throated loons nesting in the same general area. As with the red-throated loons near Storbersen, these loons also regularly flew to the ocean to fish because the small tundra lakes which the red-throated loons nested on usually did not have adequate food supplies. The researchers did witness some red-throated thievery. When they could get away with it, red-throated loons would sneak into lakes owned by the much larger yellow-billed loons to fish until discovered.

Studying red-throated loons on the island of Unst, the northernmost of the Shetland Islands off Scotland, Graham Bundy uncovered habits similar to those exhibited by Alaskan red-throated loons. In 1973 and 1974, he observed

PHOTO BY STEPHEN KRASEMANN/DRK PHOTO

twenty-four pairs living in freshwater lochs. Averaging about two acres in size, these small Scottish lakes provided little food, forcing the red-throated loons to feed almost exclusively at sea. Bundy determined the incubation period to be twenty-four to twenty-nine days. The young red-throated loons had restless wings. Bundy watched the first loon leave the lochs at the tender age of only thirty-nine days; the oldest bird to leave was forty-eight days old. By contrast, young common loons cannot fly to their own waters until they are about eighty days old.

While any bird can make a mistake, one pair of red-throated loons made a dandy. For several days in the summer of 1934, R. A. and Hazel Johnson watched a pair of red-throated loons sit faithfully on their nest. These Quebec birds were nesting well into August before the Johnsons ended the game. The loons might have sat a long time. The Johnsons found a spiral-shaped sea shell about the size of

a loon egg in the nest. It had failed to hatch.

According to most bird books, the red-throated loon is a quiet bird, but some researchers dispute that contention. Red-throated loons certainly were not quiet in 1887 when Edward W. Nelson visited Alaska; he heard red-throated calls ringing "out over the marshes twenty four hours a day during the breeding season." He also attempted a spelling of their most common call—"Gr-r-ga, gr-r-ga, ga, gr-r."

With migration routes along both the Atlantic and Pacific coasts, red-throated loons are more common in winter along the northern Atlantic coast where gatherings of a hundred or more are not unusual. Migrants have been observed far inland as well, making the red-throated the one of the "other three" loon species which most often turns up on amateur birders' life lists.

The red-throated loon's scientific name, *stellata*, is Latin meaning "starred," referring to the white speckling of the winter plumage. Other common names for the red-throated loon are equally descriptive, including the little loon, uninspired but accurate; the pegging-awl loon, a reference to the loon's bill which resembles awls used in shoe making; pepper-shinned loon, referring to the speckling on the plumage by the bird's legs; the sprat loon, a reference to the small herring called sprat which are a favorite red-throated prey; and the rain-goose, a name given by the residents of the Shetland Islands who believed the red-throated loon's calling predicted stormy weather.

Yellow-billed loon, *Gavia adamsii*

The yellow-billed loon could be called the king of the loon family. Its weight of ten to fourteen pounds is nearly three times the weight of the average red-throated loon and twice the weight of the arctic loon. Found in Eurasia, from Finland to Siberia, and in North America, from northern Alaska to the west side of Hudson's Bay, the yellow-billed loon is truly a bird of the far north, nesting only north of the tree line. In winter it migrates to coastal waters along southern Alaska and British Columbia, although some are seen occasionally down the California coast as far south as the Baja Peninsula.

Except for its large size and its pale yellow, slightly upturned bill, the yellow-billed is nearly a carbon copy of the common loon, but close inspection of yellow-billed loons shows much wider white bands in the necklace and larger but fewer white markings on the back. The winter plumage is very similar to a common loon's, with slightly lighter markings on the head and neck. The bill, even in winter, is much lighter in color and provides the best identification tag, except in the case of young yellow-billed loons which cannot be easily distinguished from the young of the common loon. The nests of the yellow-billed aid in identification. They are constructed of mounds of mud and are much larger than the nests of common loons.

The calls of the yellow-billed are harsh yet analogous to some of the common loon's calls. There is an equivalent of the wail and the yodel, and a variation of the tremolo that is even wilder and more raucous than that of the common loon. Despite published reports that yellow-billed loons call less frequently than the common, one researcher, Jeri Schwerin of Duluth, Minnesota, believes yellow-billed loons are very vocal birds. The remoteness of their breeding areas, she contends, accounts for their unearned reputation as quiet birds.

Bryan Sage studied the yellow-billed loon (also known as white-billed loon to some researchers) in arctic Alaska in 1969 and 1970. He reported that the breeding distribution of this species is entirely north of the Arctic Circle, where it nests in treeless tundra on low-rimmed freshwater lakes of forty acres or larger. He referred to the bird as an "exceedingly wary species when nesting." Sage found some overlap in distribution of the yellow-billed with the common and arctic loons.

The yellow-billed loon was named *Gavia adamsii* in honor of Edward Adams, an English surgeon-naturalist, who served on a 19th century voyage to the Arctic. Presumably he saw a few yellow-billed loons to earn the honor.

Common Loon, *Gavia immer*

The common loon is the well known loon of North America, inhabiting a breeding range from Alaska and Canada down to the northern tier of states. It has captured the interest of many scientists and the hearts of thousands of lakeside admirers. It deserves a closer look.

A Close Look

"The loon is a paragon of beauty. Alert, supple, vigorous, one knows himself to be in the presence of the master wild thing when he comes upon a loon on guard in his native element."

—W. L. Dawson, 1923

In appearance, voice, behavior and physiology, the common loon is a fascinating bird. It is distinctive from its dagger-like beak right down to its feet—they are enormous and seriously under-studied. In thousands of pages of research papers on loons, there are only casual references to the feet, usually noting simply that the feet are webbed and large. Large doesn't do justice to the loon's primary means of aquatic locomotion.

Loon devotees might want to take matters into their own hands and measure the feet of a few mounted specimens. If they did, they would find the average loon foot to be about five inches long by three inches wide. If real loon fanatics travelled to Concord, New Hampshire and visited the offices of the New Hampshire Audubon Society, they would be rewarded. A monster loon is on display there with feet nearly six inches long and a full four inches wide. (Pull out a ruler and take a careful look at four inches.) The loon is an avian bigfoot; a proportionate human shoe size would be about 45 triple R.

Swimming and Diving

While loon's feet are fully webbed with three toes, they are not what scientists call perfect swimming feet, a distinction reserved for birds like the cormorants and pelicans which have totipalmate feet (four toes joined by webs). Not perfect maybe, but the loon's feet do the job well. In the 1917 edition *Birds of America*, contributing editor Edward Howe Forbush, compared the dive of the loon to a bolt shot from a crossbow, and described their quickness as "truly astonishing."

Part of the loon's quickness is due to basic anatomy. The bird's torpedo shape, with leg muscles blending into a streamlined body mass, helps to give the loon amazing aquatic freedom. On a quiet, glassy lake surface, loons swim effortlessly, as if friction were not a physical property. Swimming with the ease of an otter, a loon bobs slightly as the big feet push alternately. Moving and at rest, loons ride low in the water with the water line just below the top of the white breast feathers, maybe two inches from the dramatic necklace.

Contrary to many reports of early naturalists, contemporary loon researchers believe that loons use only their feet for propulsion when diving and use their wings just for help in underwater turning maneuvers. This foot/wing debate has been cooled with the advent of underwater photography: several filmed sequences of diving loons show clearly the legs-only style of underwater swimming. During dives, the feet kick synchronously with powerful thrusts. According to Sigurd Olson, who in the 1950s did pioneering loon research at the University of Minnesota, this is not true for chicks. He often observed chicks trying to use their wings in diving attempts. With their buoyant down feathers, chicks need a lot of help to get down under.

How deep do common loons really dive? This simple question still sparks heated discussion among loon experts, professional and amateur alike. In 1950, Olson interviewed Lake Superior fishermen who claimed they found loons in their gill nets which had been set at depths of 240 feet. While such reports are too numerous to ignore, they are also hard to swallow. Fishermen are not known for veracity. At 200 feet the pressure is six times the normal sea level pressure, far more than most air-breathing animals can tolerate. Having unique half-bird/half-fish attributes, the loon is not like most animals. If any top-side critter could function at 200 feet, the loon is the one.

How long loons stay underwater is a related question. Probably every loon watcher has watched a loon dive and never come up. While observing loons on a small bay of Burntside Lake near Ely, Minnesota, I was amazed once when I "lost" my loon. While timing feeding dives, I watched the loon submerge. About five minutes later, I started to think I was timing a record dive. Ten minutes later, I was worried about the loon. Fifteen minutes later, I realized that the only record at stake was my gullibility. Loons are sneaky. They can surface quickly and dive again with barely a trace

of broken water, and with their rapid underwater movements, they also cover great distances in a short time. My loon, I'm sure, slipped around a point with a single underwater swim.

The scientific literature does have references to extended dives. In 1913, F. R. Jourdain reported several cases of immersion of ten minutes and one case of a wounded loon which stayed submerged for fifteen minutes, but these were extreme cases involving birds in a state of panic. When pushed to the edge of survival, many animals display extraordinary toughness, and loons are particularly tenacious. In his 1924 book, *Birds of the Lake Umbagog Region of New Hampshire*, William Brewster described the strength of a wounded loon:" . . . the heavy bullet passed directly through the middle of the neck, about three inches above the body, partially shattering some of the vertebrae and cutting the jugular vein, yet she [the loon] dove twice . . . going each time a long distance."

Most dives are quite brief. P. K. Kinnear, a British researcher watching common loons feeding on the ocean wintering range near Tronda, off the Shetland Islands, estimated the median dive at ninety seconds but did record several dives of up to five minutes. Carter, another British researcher, estimated the median feeding dive to be about twenty seconds. Of 258 dives, Carter recorded only three over one minute with the longest ninety seconds. Sigurd Olson estimated an undisturbed loon's average feeding dive at about forty seconds and timed no dives over three minutes. The length of dives is affected by several variables, but particularly the availability of prey. Why dive to a hundred feet when most prey, small fish and minnows, are usually near the surface?

The questions of depth and length of dives are illuminated by "Dewar's Rule", a rule-of-thumb estimate of time required for diving birds to get under water. The rule, proposed by John M. Dewar in 1924, states diving birds need twenty seconds for the first six feet of a dive and ten seconds for each additional six foot increment. The journey to 200 feet would take a loon about six minutes. Of course the loon has to get back to the surface which would require probably an additional three or four minutes, placing a loon at the very edge of any reported immersion times. Animals rarely subject themselves to such danger, especially when so little is at stake. While loons certainly dive to depths in excess of a hundred feet, their dives to 200 feet, supported only by the claims of commercial fishermen, should be viewed with healthy skepticism.

While the maximum depths and durations of dives are not well documented, the physiological mechanisms the loon utilizes to make extended dives are fairly well understood. Over a hundred years ago, W. H. Slaney advanced the theory that diving birds could change their specific grav-

ity (the weight of an object divided by the weight of an equal volume of water) by expelling air from their body cavities. His contemporaries studying divers believed birds like the gallinule remained underwater by grasping vegetation with their feet. Slaney was right. To prepare for dives, loons expel air from their body and compress their dense and waterproof plumage tightly, forcing out air trapped between vanes of the feathers. With these air reduction techniques, loons can sink into the water without noticeable effort.

Just getting rid of unwanted air does not make a bird a great diver; several other important physiological adaptations help the loon earn its nickname of "the great northern diver." Fifty years ago noted ornithologist Erwin Stresemann described the loon's skeleton as completely lacking

Adult common loon "running" on water before taking flight.
PHOTO BY DAVE REPP

pneumaticity. While typical bird bones have an interior sponge-like construction with lots of air spaces (a lightweight skeletal construction ideal for organisms adapted for flight), the loon is not typical; it is built for diving first and flying second. Since any air within the body cavity, even in the bones, would compromise diving abilities, the evolutionary path for the loon went the way of water and favored the development of many solid bones in the skeleton, which made diving much easier but flying a little tougher.

Another significant adaptation of loons is their ability to dive with minimal oxygen. While underwater, loons derive needed oxygen from the oxyhemoglobin and oxymyoglobin stored in the blood and muscles. According to A. W. Schorger, the dark color of the flesh of diving birds, including loons, is due to the presence of these respiratory pigments. In addition, the loon's circulatory system helps by reducing the heart rate.

The loon's vital body organs have an unusual tolerance for low levels of oxygen. In the textbook *Avian Biology*, edited by Donald Farner and James King, this phenomenon is described as a system which rations available oxygen preferentially to tissues particularly susceptible to damage from oxygen deprivation. Farner and King report a ninety-percent metabolic reduction during experimental submergence of some diving ducks. While such tests have not been performed on loons, it is likely that similar metabolic reductions occur. Like most birds, loons normally have a high metabolic rate which is reflected in their body temperature of about 102°F.

Age

With their internal motors running at such high speeds, it's surprising loons live as long as they do. While definitive answers await additional banding research, most scientists believe the common loon is "long-lived." While an arctic loon was recovered eighteen years after banding and a red-throated loon in Sweden was found twenty-three years after banding, no common loons of that age have been recovered, even though 587 have been banded. Yet, biologists estimate the life span of the common loon at fifteen to thirty years.

Many familiar birds live much longer. Wild Canada geese often live over twenty years. Golden eagles in the wild can reach thirty, while eagles of several other species have survived fifty years of captivity. Herring gulls, thought by some to be distantly related to loons, can live twenty years, and some captive gulls have reached forty. If a common loon is found wearing a thirty-year-old band, few people will be surprised.

Size

The common loon is a large bird. In most bird books the weight range is listed as seven to nine pounds. Weighing a number of loons from Alberta, Canadian Wildlife Service researcher Kees Vermeer found their average weight to be eight pounds. The largest male weighed nearly eleven pounds and the largest female weighed just over eight pounds. The U.S. Fish and Wildlife Service weighed eight loons killed by botulism. Found in Lake Michigan, these birds weighed in from eight to just under thirteen pounds. While most scientists agree that males are larger, the difference is slight and does not provide an accurate method for field identification.

There is substantial evidence for a geographical size gradient. The smallest loons reside in Minnesota, North Dakota and Manitoba, averaging about nine pounds. Much larger common loons live in the Northeast, averaging about twelve pounds. Baffin Island is home to the largest loons.

Because their bodies are compact and dense, loons are deceptively heavy. While the bald eagle appears to be much larger than the loon, eagles weigh eight to twelve pounds, just slightly heavier than the average common loon. Sandhill cranes, with wingspreads of seven feet, have an average weight about the same as the common loon.

The length of common loons ranges from twenty-eight to thirty-five inches. Thirteen adult loons from Minnesota had an average length of twenty-nine inches.

Flight

Even with a large wingspan of up to fifty-eight inches, common loons still have a body weight disproportionate to their wing area. Olson compared the loon's wing area with its weight and found the ratio to be 0.5 compared to a 8.87 ratio for the golden crowned kinglet. While this doesn't mean that it is seventeen times easier for the kinglet to get off the ground, it does reveal the loon's flying handicap. In his book *Birds of the World*, Oliver Austin underscored this point by observing that loons have the " . . . least wing surface in proportion to their body weight of any flying bird." In 1957, researcher D. B. Savile graphically described the loon's flight: "The common loon is a flying anachronism. It has an appallingly high wing load and very inefficient wing form . . . it takes off only with great difficulty, after a long run and climbs shallowly."

How long is that run? While loons sometimes need up to a quarter mile of aquatic runway, they can be more efficient. In his classic *Handbook of North American Birds*, Ralph S. Palmer reports common loons taking off after a twenty-yard run. While wind is a factor, it is not needed (contrary to loon folklore) to get the birds off the water. One calm summer day in northern Wisconsin, I watched a pair of loons take off from a small lake, marking the distance with prominent landmarks. Later, using detailed maps of the lake, I estimated the distance from the first "step" to breaking contact with water at about eighty yards. There are probably many variables involved here, but the individual loon's capability is, no doubt, the most important one.

Getting off the water, however, does not get a loon safely away from the lake. The ascent of a loon's flight is quite gradual, often forcing the bird to circle a lake to get over the treetops. On many small lakes, loons fall into routine flight patterns, curving around part of the lake and heading over the trees at a fairly predictable spot. When flying, the feet are extended straight back and held close together. The flight is not silent.

On a canoe trip in Ontario's Quetico Provincial Park, my wife, Pat, and I were on the water at dawn on a foggy morning when a pair of loons flew toward us just a few feet off the water. About fifty feet from the canoe, they flared slightly to our left and passed us at eye level only fifteen feet from the canoe. In twenty years of camping and canoeing in loon country, I had never been so close to flying loons, or so awed by any natural sight or sound. The wings cutting through the air created a sound much louder and more dramatic than the whistling of mallard wings or that of any other bird I've heard. Unlike those of other large birds like geese, cranes or herons, a loon's wing beats are very rapid, about 250 beats per minute.

The speed of flying loons is surprisingly fast. While most bird books still list the common loon's flight speed at 60 mph, contemporary researchers place the speed substantially higher. New York biologist Paul Kurlinger has estimated ground speeds (taking into account following winds) of 93 mph during spring migration and 108 mph during fall migration. The average air speed (not counting the help of wind) was 75 mph. A physician flying his airplane near Charlotte, North Carolina, had his small plane at nearly full throttle while watching a loon pull away. He estimated the loon's speed at 100 mph.

Arthur Cleveland Bent, in his *Life Histories of North American Diving Birds*, was superbly expressive describing the loon's flight:

> "The lines are perfect; the strong neck and breast, terminating in the long sharp bill, are outstretched to pierce the air like the keenest spear; the heavy body, tapering fore and aft, glides through the air with the

PHOTO BY WOODY HAGGE

least possible resistance; and the big feet, held close together and straight out behind, form an effective rudder. The flight of a loon is decidedly distinctive; such a rakish craft, long and pointed at both ends, could not be mistaken for anything else.''

It's obvious Bent did not have a graduate school committee looking over his shoulder; his rich prose is a rarity in scientific literature.

A loon's transition from air to water is nearly as exciting as that from water to air. Described by Olson as graceful, perfect seaplane touch-downs, loon landings begin with a long set-wing glide before their landing gear drops to drag the water for a short distance and end with full braking with their breasts. If there is a wind, loons, like all waterfowl, will land into it.

Not all landings are picture perfect. Some loon watchers have witnessed total wipeouts. Paul Strong, a biologist from the University of Maine, has seen some dandies with wings, legs and neck going in several directions at once. Coming in as fast as they do, even minor landing errors can provide comic relief. Loons often dive immediately after landing, perhaps to check the area for danger. After a quick underwater exploration, loons surface and usually perform a couple of wing flaps before settling down.

Molting

Feathers do not last a loon's lifetime: they simply wear out with use. The striking plumage of the adult loon requires constant care and periodic replacement of old feathers. Molting, the annual or bi-annual process of natural feather loss and replacement, is usually related to the breeding cycle. Most ducks, after hatching their eggs, go through a complete molt, including flight feathers, which provides new feathers for the fall migration. While biologists believe molting is hormonally controlled, they have not isolated the precise control mechanism. Many birds undergo head and

A September adult common loon in the early stages of molting.
PHOTO BY DAVE REPP

A molting loon caught in the act. Note the "white face"—molting usually starts on the chin and neck.
PHOTO BY DAVE REPP

body molt during nesting season and a flight feather molt after migration. For other birds, like the red-wing blackbird, both the extent and the timing of the molt vary by region. Since the variations seem endless, most scientists suspect there is not a common molting scheme among birds.

During his 1950 study of common loons on lakes in the northern Minnesota canoe country, Sigurd Olson carefully observed the common loon's molting process. He noticed the earliest signs of the molt in late August. By then he found patches of breast and back feathers on the water. Because the ends of the feathers were concave instead of pointed, he knew the feathers were pushed out by new ones. He watched loons molt first at the base of the bill, the chin and forehead and later on the back. In early September he noted only one gray-faced bird, but by mid-September nearly all the loons showed some signs of molt. By late September most birds were in complete winter plumage. When Olson paddled out of his wilderness study area in early October, he saw no loons in the black and white breeding plumage. At this time the adults, now in winter plumage, were difficult to distinguish from their young.

The exact time of the fall molt appears to vary. In Maine, Paul Strong has observed loons in breeding plumage as late as December. In New Hampshire loon plumage typically starts to change in late October and early November. Rawson Wood, one of New Hampshire's most avid loon watchers, cannot recall seeing any birds in breeding plumage after November. Most Wisconsin loon watchers, even those living on lakes with resident loons, rarely see a loon in winter plumage. Even birds leaving Wisconsin in late November, when most lakes freeze, are clearly black and white. It is possible, but not likely, that all of the late-leaving loons are the young-of-the-year and that adults in breeding plumage all leave much earlier.

According to ornithologist Gene Woolfenden, the common loon's wing molt takes place in late winter on coastal waters. His evidence is a number of loons found without wing feathers during February on Florida beaches. This delayed wing molt, Woolfenden suggests, relates to the degree of parental care loons provide their young. To feed and protect their chicks, loons need to be mobile and consequently need their wing feathers. Protecting their territory is vital to a loon and covering up to 200 acres of water often demands flight. If the flight feathers were replaced after the young were fairly independent, migration of the adults could be greatly delayed and loons would then face the possibility of an early freeze and premature death. Evolution doesn't work that way; loons play it safe, keeping their wing feathers through the fall migration.

Another factor in the delayed molt is the energy cost of replacing large flight feathers. Depending upon the species, the energy cost of molting is anywhere from five to

Common loon doing a "rolling preen." Note the out-stretched foot. Often loons at rest will extend and wiggle one of their feet. This "foot waggle" could be a stretching exercise or an attempt to pickup heat by exposing the foot to sunlight. Or could it be "loon yoga"? PHOTO BY DAVE REPP

thirty percent of total daily energy demand. Molting plus concurrent caring for young would place considerable stress on parent loons. According to Woolfenden, immature loons spend two or three winters on the coast before returning to northern waters. During their adolescence on the coast, they replace their wing feathers in late summer or early fall, not in winter as the adults do. Since these immature loons have no young to provide for, nor ice-covered lakes to worry about, there is no reason for them to delay their molt.

Red-throated loons are the exception to the adult loon delayed wing molt rule. They have a complete post-nuptial molt in summer. Because the red-throated loons do not face the same "ice-in" danger (they can lift right off the water, not requiring a long running start) they can afford to wait until ice cover is nearly complete before heading south. Common loons, as well as arctic and yellow-billed loons, do not have that luxury.

Care of Feathers

To date no enterprising graduate student has counted the feathers on a loon, but researchers have estimated the number of feathers on some birds. We know at least one whistling swan had 25,216 feathers and one house sparrow 3,500. The loon probably falls somewhere in between the two in the feather count.

Whatever the number, the feathers of the loon in large part account for the bird's celebrity status. The stark simplicity of the black and white design give this ancient bird a modern look. Unlike loons, many bird species have separate dress codes for males and females. Usually the plumage differences, as with ducks or pheasants, are permanent, but some birds like the scarlet tanager or indigo bunting have seasonal differences. Creating much confusion for researchers, loons have identical, not just similar, breeding plumage. One loon is as beautiful as the next, which makes field identification of individuals very tricky.

PHOTO BY WOODY HAGGE

To keep their feathers looking good, loons spend a lot of time preening. Removing external parasites and distributing oil from a gland at the base of the tail, preening is vital for survival. A few avian species, including some parrots, pigeons and herons indulge in reciprocal preening. This "you scratch my back and I'll scratch yours" behavior is most common with pairs that spend a lot of time together at the nest site. Except for the short periods when trading incubation duties, loons are alone at the nest, and they are solo preeners. In winter, loons spend about twenty percent of their daylight hours preening and performing other maintenance activity. During molt periods additional time is invested in feather care. Surprisingly, preening can be exciting to watch.

In late August of 1984, I spent a full day watching a pair of adults and an immature loon on a northern Wisconsin lake which was small enough to allow observation from a single position. (A twenty-power spotting scope and tripod helped.) The birds went about their rather routine feeding, resting and preening activities until mid-afternoon, when the immature bird went totally berserk in an orgy of preening. The loon repeatedly rolled on its back, kicked its legs in the air, splashed with its wings and all the while preened aggressively. The show lasted two hours but included a few well-deserved rest breaks. Meanwhile the adults were also preening vigorously but without the theatrics of rolling on their backs. After the performance I went to the windward shoreline. With a stiff wind blowing, I didn't have long to wait before a trail of feathers hit the beach. This was serious preening. Apparently such wild preening behavior is not limited to the common loon. Near Point Barrow, in northern Alaska, Jeri Schwerin observed yellow-billed loons preening with the same roll-on-the-back intensity.

A Curious Creature

Common loons are a curious lot. Even during the era when loons were favored targets, Bent noticed that common loons could not resist the impulse to investigate. He found it was "an easy matter to toll [attract] one within gunshot range by remaining hidden and waving some suspicious object." I've tested Bent's theory on several occasions and discovered that loons have not learned much over the past sixty-five years: they are still gullible. Once I brought two adults and a chick within a distance of ten feet from shore by waving a spruce branch and giving a ridiculously inept version of the "hoot" call. Two less than quiet dogs were at my feet and even their low growling did not suppress the loons' powerful curiosity.

Loons are not graceful all the time. PHOTO BY DAVE REPP

Yellow-billed loons are equally curious. In 1943, A. M. Bailey made an expedition to arctic Alaska where he encountered yellow-billed loons willing to check him out when he loudly yelled "yoo hoo" and frantically waved a cloth. In the dark days of the turn of the century, when loons were shot for sport, this instinct to know what's going on in their territories probably shortened the lives of many loons.

The Red Eye

A look at the common loon is not complete without reference to the bird's dramatic red eye, a feature shared by the other three species of loons. Without the ruby eye, fewer artists would be inspired to capture the loon on canvas. Always a source of romantic mystery, the loon's bright red eye raises the obvious question—why red? The way to approach the question is through a better question—why is the loon's eye not some other color? According to biologist Denny Olson who conducted research on light penetration of water at the Minnesota Zoo, red may be a lesser evil which was selected by default. Scientists have known for some time, he explains, that water filters out the red, orange and yellow end of the spectrum first, allowing the blues and violets to penetrate deeper into a lake.

Because a loon's eye reflects red light back to us, it looks red. By reflecting red light, a loon's eye eliminates red light before it enters the eye; in effect, it does the same thing as the water—it eliminates red. If a loon's eye were blue, it would filter out the only light available for deepwater fishing. Beyond fifteen feet or so there is no red any-

way, so why not have an eye that filters out red? Any other color would remove even more light, making fishing tougher. A small but perhaps important added advantage of the red eye could be the camouflage effect of an eye that appears gray at depths of fifteen feet or deeper, which would not reflect back to alert prey fish. Scientifically, this is a solid explanation, but don't tell any artists or poets.

A Nameless Star

Because enjoying loons is usually part of larger experiences, it's difficult to summarize the attraction of the common loon. Writing in the June, 1947 issue of *The Living Wilderness*, Olaus J. Murie, one of the founders of the Wilderness Society and an enduring wilderness philosopher, captured with sublime understatement the importance of loons:

> "We returned to camp in the evening. The wind was dying down as the sun sank below the trees. The sky was saffron when the moon climbed into view and a large bright star dropped its reflection with that of the moon on the still, darkening water while from out in the lake arose the exuberant yodeling of loons. We stood in the deepening dusk, reverently. I did not want to speculate on what star that was. A man-made name would be an intrusion here. I wanted only to look and feel and listen, while the saffron tint faded, the shoreline shadows darkened, the moon and that glorious star gradually took over their place of prominence in the night. Long after we had crept into the tents and lay quiet and contented in our sleeping bags, we listened to the wild serenading of the loons."

PHOTO BY WOODY HAGGE

Status and Distribution

*"A pair of loons nested in Quittacus Pond, Lakeville, Massachusetts, about fourteen
miles from my home, in 1872, but the eggs were taken and both birds were shot; none
have nested in this section of the state since. The same story is true of many other
New Hampshire lakes where the insatiable desire to kill has forever extirpated an
exceedingly interesting bird."*

—Arthur Cleveland Bent, 1919

An accurate image of the common loon's status in
North America would not be a snapshot of the current geographic breeding range, but rather a motion picture cap-
turing the northward progression of the loon's "permanent"
range. It would not be an entirely pleasant film, especially
the frames from the early twentieth century when the retreat
northward was shockingly rapid.

Historical Perspective

Little is known about the distribution of loons prior to
European settlement. While references to loons are frequent
in Native American legends, geographical or population de-
terminations based upon these references are speculative at
best. It is probably safe to assume that in the presettlement
era common loons bred over much of the Northeast, Midwest and Pacific Northwest of the United States and nearly
all of Canada except the arctic regions. It is also probably
safe to assume that loons in seventeenth century America

were at or near their maximum biological carrying capacity
in most of their range. Although some Indian tribes har-
vested loons for food, others protected the loon as part of
their religious traditions; human-caused mortality of loons
was minimal.

The southern edge of loon country started to move
north in the late eighteenth and early nineteenth centuries.
In that time the shooting of loons was considered great
sport. William Brewster described well the attitude toward
loons by observing in a 1924 publication: " . . . it was cus-
tomary to shoot at them [loons] whenever opportunity offered." Many people looked for the opportunity. "That was
an era," explains Jeff Fair of New Hampshire's loon recovery program, "in which our society had gunpowder and the
time to play with it, but too little environmental understanding or conscience to realize the effects of such behavior."

In 1912, Edward H. Forbush described in detail recreational loon shoots in Buzzards Bay and Manomet Bay,

Massachusetts. On a breezy spring day, these popular loon shooting spots would be filled with boats carrying hunters eager to measure their wing shooting skills by their success in hitting fast-flying loons. Most of the loon mortality in this era probably resulted from the thousands of less public incidents: a bored duck hunter wondering if the old story about loons being faster than bullets were true . . . a sport fisherman thinking the loons on his pond were stealing trout . . . market hunters firing indiscriminately at any group of waterbirds. Whatever their method or motive, the shotgunners changed the loon's distribution and status. Even as far north as Maine loons began to disappear. By the 1920s on Maine's Lake Umbagog, loons were scarce.

By the time systematic natural history surveys were conducted, the loons' southern limit had already been transposed some distance to the north. But at the turn of the century loons were still more common than they are today. In the 1895 volume of *The Ornithology of Illinois,* Robert Ridgeway described the common loon as a " . . . common winter resident on larger waters throughout the state", which nested "in the northern portion."

In the 1917 edition of *Birds of America,* T. Gilbert Pearson listed the common loon's breeding range as the area "south to parallel 42°." This designation included northern Illinois; the northern half of Iowa; all of Wisconsin, Michigan, Minnesota, the Dakotas, Montana, Washington; the northern fringe of Pennsylvania and Connecticut; and all of the Northeast. Bent's 1919 *Life Histories of North American Diving Birds* put the breeding line in roughly the same place, but referred specifically to central Pennsylvania, northeastern Indiana, northeastern Illinois, northern Iowa, and northeastern California to describe the southern edge of the common loon's breeding range. Loons were still relatively abundant, prompting Bent to comment that "nearly every suitable lake within the breeding range of the species has its pair of loons, or has had it, and many lakes support two or more pairs."

The Migratory Bird Treaty Act of 1918 helped to hold the line. The provisions of the act controlled the previously unregulated harvest of waterbirds, but some biologists think the law came too late; the damage to the loon's reproductive capacity, especially in the East, had already been severe. And many of the blessings of the twentieth century, such as massive habitat destruction, chemical contamination, and oil spills were yet to come.

The Common Loon in the 1980s

In the nearly seven decades since Bent described the loon's breeding range many problems more serious for loons than birdshot have emerged. Lakeshore development has had probably the most devastating consequences. Except in northern Maine and in the large federal tracts in northern Minnesota, lakes without a necklace of summer homes are hard to find these days. The post-World War II economic boom, coupled with a new interest in the outdoors, fueled an all-out assault on our northern lakes.

I learned this history lesson in July of 1959 during my first fishing trip to northern Wisconsin. I was twelve years old and could think of little else but muskies as long as an oar. There were no superhighways then from my hometown of Sun Prairie, Wisconsin to the Lac du Flambeau fishing paradise in Vilas County, nearly three hundred miles north. With no extra lanes or bypasses, it seemed to take forever to drive through Wausau, a modest city even now.

What I had expected to find and what I found when I arrived in the "north" were quite different. My childhood fantasies of wild country brimming with fish and wildlife collided violently with the reality of countless lakeside developments, backwoods intersections cluttered with a bewildering array of resort and supperclub signs, commercialized Indian ceremonials and ubiquitous bait shops hyping minnows "Guaranteed to Catch Fish or Die Trying." For northern Wisconsin, the decade of the 50s was the beginning of the end for authentic wilderness. No one was counting loons then, but as nest sites became beaches, boat docks or picnic grounds, loons were gradually pushed to remote lake corners until the necklace of whitewashed cabins became a noose choking off the last breath of wildness. Yet, loons did not disappear from all of Wisconsin's northern lakes. Many adapted to their new neighbors, and a sizable population still calls Wisconsin home. But the lakes are different now, and life for the remaining loons is . . . well, who can say?

This pattern of lakeshore development on northern lakes was similar in most loon states. In some areas of the Northeast, the lot sizes were larger and more homes sported redwood or cedar siding, but the overall effect was the same: loons had to share their lakes with many more people. While hard data on loon populations between 1950 and 1980 are limited, it is clear that during that period loon numbers in most of the United States declined substantially. Speaking at the 1979 North American Conference on Common Loon Research and Management, Richard Plunkett of the National Audubon Society confirmed what many lakeshore observers believed when he noted that "Available data from Minnesota, Wisconsin, Michigan, New York, Vermont, New Hampshire, Massachusetts and Maine suggest a northward shrinkage of the historically occupied breeding range of the common loon." No substantial breeding populations of loons now exist south of central Vermont or central New Hampshire. Only a few pairs nest in Massachusetts, and no loons breed anymore in Pennsylvania, Connecticut or Rhode Island.

While loss of habitat is the primary factor in the decline of the common loon, the problems of harassment of nesting loons, deterioration of water quality, disease, and oil spills on coastal wintering areas have all contributed to the gradual reduction of the United States' common loon breeding population. Rawson Wood, Chairman of the North American Loon Fund, captured the current status of the loon in

a single sentence: "The breeding range of this extraordinary bird—long the symbol of north country wilderness—has been shrinking wherever people have brought boats to its lakes and camps to the shorelines." Loons can exist with people, but both the loons and the people have to work at it. The people especially.

The effects of development become clear when wilderness areas are surveyed for loon populations. In areas where solitude is still a characteristic of the lake environment, loons continue to do well. In northern Minnesota over ninety percent of the lakes fifty acres or larger support breeding loons. In Ontario's Quetico Provincial Park, nearly every lake has a pair or two. In remote areas of western Ontario, loons are still at their maximum biological carrying capacity.

Official Status

Officially, the common loon is not an endangered species. Unlike the California condor, the peregrine falcon, or the Kirtland's warbler, the common loon is not on the U.S. Department of Interior's *List of Endangered Wildlife*. The federal designation process for *endangered species* requires that the species be "in danger of extinction throughout all or a significant portion of its range." The same holds for federally *threatened species*; the species must be "likely within the foreseeable future to become endangered throughout all or part of a significant portion of its range."

The key word is significant. Loons are in serious trouble in parts of their range, but not in a large enough percentage to fit the endangered or threatened criteria; therefore, the special protections and funding programs of the Endangered Species Act are not available for loon management efforts. In 1984, the U.S. Fish and Wildlife Service did nominate the common loon for a new *List of National Species of Special Emphasis*, but Congress did not accept the nomination. Technically, the common loon has no special

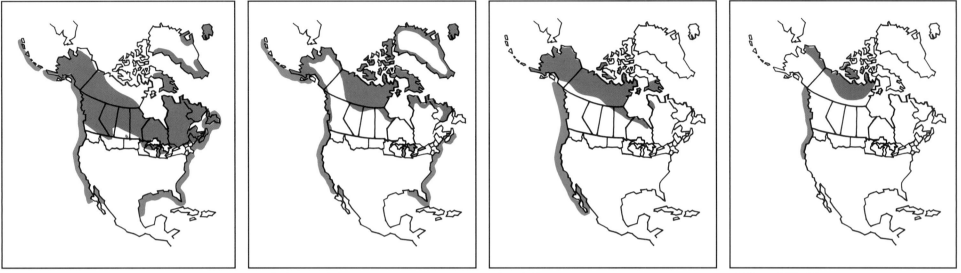

Common Loon   Red-throated Loon   Arctic Loon   Yellow-billed Loon

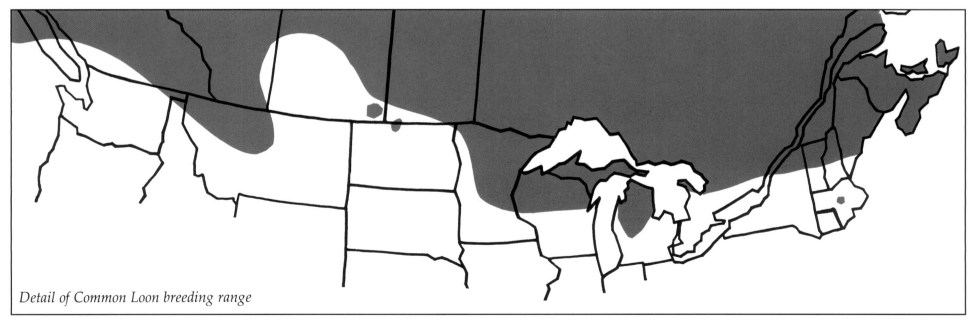

Detail of Common Loon breeding range

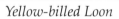

■ Wintering Range
■ Breeding Range

status, but according to Mark Schaefer, coordinator of the U.S. Fish and Wildlife Service's Non-Game office, there is "some concern" within the federal office and special management attention for loons is likely. He also noted that a joint U.S.-Canadian report on the status of the common loon is in the works.

At the state level there has been a lot of attention directed toward common loon management and many states have provided special designations. For example, it has been declared by state legislation a *threatened species* in New Hampshire. In Wisconsin, the loon is on the state's *Watch List,* indicating that a close monitoring of the species is needed. The picture of loons in the United States today is a mosaic with pockets of plenty like northern Minnesota, states with marginal populations like Vermont, and states like Wisconsin with fairly comfortable numbers.

UNITED STATES

Maine

Official State Classification: None
The Non-Game office of the Maine Department of Inland Fisheries and Wildlife is presently developing a classification system for non-game species.

Historical Perspective:
No population data were generated before the Maine Audubon Society started a statewide survey in 1977. The survey, utilizing volunteer observers, uncovered comments from old-timers indicating that any dramatic decline in loon numbers must have occurred "many years ago." Loon populations in the southern half of the state have declined during the twentieth century. While historical records indicate that loons once bred in every county of the state, loons presently do not breed in several southern counties.

Present Population:
Jane Arbuckle, wildlife director of the Maine Audubon Society, estimates the population in Maine at close to 4,000 loons. Since Maine has only 2,700 lakes greater than ten acres in size, the estimate reflects a high density of loons. The 1984 survey conducted jointly by the Maine Audubon Society and the Maine Cooperative Wildlife Research Unit at Orono included ground and aerial observations. Based on the survey, officials estimated the 1984 population at a minimum of 3,531 loons.

Prospects:
Arbuckle considers the loon population to be "healthy," particularly in Maine's northern half. She is generally optimistic about the loon's future in Maine. She feels the conversion of many summer camps into year-round homes is a plus for loons because permanent residents in the lake environment are likely "to take more responsibility for their lake and their loons." While Arbuckle would like to see more hard data, she points to the loon research at the University of Maine in Orono, conducted by the Department of Interior's Cooperative Wildlife Research Unit, as a source of vital new information for loon management.

Private Loon Organizations:
The Maine Audubon Society, coordinating with the Maine Department of Inland Fisheries and Wildlife and the Maine Cooperative Wildlife Research Unit in Orono, conducts an annual survey and sponsors public education programs.

New Hampshire

Official State Classification: Threatened Species
Historical Perspective:
While estimates of former loon populations are not precise, loons once nested on at least twice as many lakes in New Hampshire as they do today. A 1977 survey of sixty-

eight lakes with historical records of loon usage turned up only thirty-two with loons, a fifty-three percent decline. Winnipesaukee, the state's largest lake, has a history of supporting thirty to forty pairs but supported only ten pairs in 1978.

The New Hampshire Loon Preservation Committee conducted the first statewide survey in 1976 and recorded a total population of 271 loons. In 1977 and 1978 the population declined slightly, but in 1981 it jumped sharply and increased steadily over the next three years.

Present Population:

The 1984 loon census turned up a total of 373 loons, the highest number since The Loon Preservation Committee (LPC) started the survey in 1976. Sixty chicks were fledged, representing a drop from the 1983 total of eighty-three. Jeff Fair, Director of the LPC, cited the 1984 spring flooding of nests as a factor in the productivity decline. He also noted a "significant increase in the number of unpaired, presumably younger adults" which, he believes, might forecast "an increase in future breeding populations."

Prospects:

Due to the effectiveness of a decade of public education and the employment of artificial nesting islands, the state's population is on the upswing. Since 1980 the number of nesting pairs has increased each year. The New Hampshire LPC, the first loon group in the United States, is actively involved in a recovery effort directed toward the re-establishment of loons throughout New Hampshire.

Private Loon Organizations:

The annual survey is conducted by The New Hampshire LPC, a project of the Audubon Society of New Hampshire.

Massachusetts

Official State Classification: State Rare

This classification requires that "all reasonable effort be made to avoid adversely affecting" the loon.

Historical Perspective:

Loons were common in Massachusetts during colonial times, but in 1905 Edward Forbush would comment that "formerly loons bred in the more remote ponds of Massachusetts." After a long absence, loons returned to Massachusetts. In 1975, a single pair took up residence on the Quabbin Reservoir. The state population trebled by 1981 when three pairs nested on the Quabbin and produced five chicks.

Present Population:

A 1984 survey conducted by Paul Lyons and Ellen Ehrhardt indicated a state population of fourteen adult common loons, including four nesting pairs on the Quabbin Reservoir (the 25,000 acre lake which comprises the domestic water supply for Boston) and one nesting pair on the 4,000 acre Wachusett Reservoir. Four chicks were fledged in 1984.

Prospects:

According to survey coordinators, the prospects for Massachusetts look good. Protection of nesting loons will continue and the publicity generated by the 1984 project should make protection programs in future years more effective. With only a handful of loons, it appears that the state has nowhere to go but up, but that depends heavily upon the rain. The only clouds on the horizon are the ones carrying acid rain. Unless improvements in the acid rain situation are made soon, the Quabbin Reservoir, according to Dick Cronin of the Massachusetts Division of Fish and Wildlife, will be acidified by 1995.

Private Loon Organizations:

The Massachusetts Audubon Society, the Massachusetts Division of Fisheries and Wildlife, and the Metropolitan District Commission jointly sponsor a conservation and management program.

Vermont

Official State Classification: State Endangered (Pending)
This classification awaits the expected approval of the Secretary of the State's Department of Environmental Conservation.

Historical Perspective:
While there are no solid historical baseline population estimates for loons in Vermont, early naturalists reported loons breeding on most of Vermont's larger lakes. Records clearly indicate loons nested on Dunmore and Bomoseen Lakes and Mallets Bay of Lake Champlain, all lakes where no loons have nested for at least thirty years. In 1978, the Vermont Institute of Natural Sciences (VINS) staff and volunteers surveyed sixty-eight lakes and found only sixteen active loon nests. A total of fifty-six adult loons were sighted.

Present Population:
The 1984 VINS survey, covering 109 lakes and involving 129 volunteers, was not encouraging. Seventeen loon pairs were observed, but only eight were nesting pairs. Most disappointing was the number of surviving chicks. Only six chicks survived into September, about half the number from earlier surveys. The poor production in 1984 was mainly attributed to wet spring nesting conditions which caused the loss of at least three nests.

Prospects:
According to Chris Fichtel, VINS loon coordinator, the state's loon population, concentrated in the northeast corner of the state, is "marginal." While the population has declined, loons are hanging on. Fichtel, for one, does not believe Vermont will lose its loons, but does believe the bird is in trouble. Though the number of territorial pairs has seen no significant decline since 1978, few new pairs have established territories—not a good sign.

Efforts to increase productivity through the use of artificial nest islands have not been successful and no chicks were hatched off the islands in 1984. An active and concerned volunteer group coordinated by VINS will play an important role in the struggle to keep loons in Vermont.

Private Loon Organizations:
The Vermont Institute of Natural Sciences conducts an annual Vermont Loon Watch Day and sponsors a wide range of public education events.

New York

Official State Classification: Species of Special Concern
This classification refers to species for which a risk of endangerment has been documented.

Historical Perspective:
There are a few records documenting early loon populations in New York State. One is an 1899 reference by E. R. Wallace to the "weird cry of the loon" in a guide to the Adirondacks. Loon researcher Judy McIntyre believes loons probably once bred on most of the Adirondack lakes, as well as on all or most of the Finger Lakes.

In 1978, a survey was conducted on eighty-five lakes with historical records of loon use. Only fifty-four of those lakes still had loons, a thirty-six percent decline. A 1979 survey of Adirondack lakes revealed 169 pairs on 302 lakes and reflected a thirty-two percent decline over fifteen years.

Present Population:
In 1983, the Adirondack Loon Preservation Project, sponsored by The Adirondack Council, estimated a population of 247 adults and eighty-two chicks. Thirty percent of the adults and forty percent of the chicks were found in Hamilton County.

Prospects:

The future of loons in New York State is tied quite closely to the acid rain issue. Over 200 Adirondack lakes are now fishless and consequently devoid of loons. Shoreline development pressure continues on some lakes and the loon population trends in New York over the past thirty years are not encouraging. Preserving loons in New York State will require considerable effort, but Anita Davis of The Adirondack Council's Loon Project sees "a tremendous amount of interest in loons," and notes that the project has a large group of eager volunteers.

Private Loon Organizations:

After initiating loon protection and survey efforts, the Adirondack Loon Preservation Project has assumed a "support" role to the New York Wildlife Committee (inspired by the New York office of the National Audubon Society) working in coordination with the New York Department of Environmental Conservation.

Michigan

Official State Classification: Watch List

Historical Perspective:

Journals of nineteenth century naturalists indicate the common loon once nested throughout Michigan, but there are no official records of historical loon distribution.

Present Population:

The loon population in Michigan is unevenly distributed. There are a few nesting loons in southwestern Michigan, in an area called by John Lerg of the Michigan Department of Natural Resources (DNR) "a pocket of wilderness" and a few more in the northern lower peninsula. However, most of the state's loon population is concentrated in the wilder Upper Peninsula. Jim Hammill of the Michigan DNR's Crystal Falls office coordinated a 1983 loon survey of the Upper Peninsula. The DNR team esti-

mated that 120 loon pairs produced 175 chicks. Hammill also provided a rough estimate of 100 loons for the Lower Peninsula and thirty loons for Michigan's Isle Royale in Lake Superior, bringing the state total to approximately 450 loons.

Prospects:

The Michigan population appears to be stable. The work of the Michigan DNR in the Upper Peninsula should insure that the loon population is closely watched.

Private Loon Organizations: None

Wisconsin

Official State Classification: Watch List

Historical Perspective:

The 1903 volume *Birds of Wisconsin* by Kumlien and Hollister listed the common loon as a common breeder northward from the southern tier of counties. The authors referred to two southern Wisconsin lakes, Lake Koshkonong near Madison and Delavan Lake near the Illinois border, as locales for breeding loons. At the turn of the century loons in northern Wisconsin were abundant. The first population survey was conducted by the Wisconsin Department of Natural Resources (DNR) in 1976.

Present Population:

Since 1978 an annual survey has been conducted by Wisconsin Project Loon Watch (WPLW), a program of the Sigurd Olson Environmental Institute of Northland College in Ashland. The population estimate for 1984, extrapolated from an actual count of 1,915 loons on 648 lakes, was 3,000 loons.

Prospects:

The population in Wisconsin appears to be increasing slightly. Although the large number of lakes in the northern half of the state complicates efforts to accurately measure the population, population surveys over ten years provide evidence that loons are returning to some lakes after decades of absence. A 1980 addition to the state statutes which clarified the definition of harassment has helped to reduce incidents of loon harassment. An aggressive public education program by WPLW and the Wisconsin DNR has fostered a public attitude supportive of loon preservation efforts.

Private Loon Organizations:

Wisconsin Project Loon Watch, in cooperation with the Wisconsin DNR, conducts an annual survey, sponsors a wide variety of public education activities and supports a modest loon research program. Over 700 volunteers are involved in the annual loon survey.

Minnesota

Official State Classification: State Bird

No management designation has been given to the common loon.

Historical Perspective:

Minnesota is one state where the common loon is common. In the 1932 edition of *Birds of Minnesota* the loon was listed as breeding throughout the state, but the editor, Thomas S. Roberts, suggested a decline was in progress: the loon was " . . . formerly much more abundant than at present when every clear water lake was the home of a pair or more of noisy loons. Its steady decrease has been due, in great part, to the fact that this large bird has been the favorite target of the man with a gun."

The Land of 10,000 Lakes has probably hosted over 10,000 loons for many years. A 1980 survey of the Minnesota Department of Natural Resources (DNR) tallied 1,367 adults and 503 chicks on just 437 lakes. Officials extrapolated a statewide total of approximately 10,000 loons. Judy McIntyre, who conducted graduate research on loons at the University of Minnesota, estimated that about eighty percent of all Minnesota lakes over fifty acres have loons.

Present Population:

State DNR officials continue to use 10,000 as an estimate of Minnesota's loon population. The northern Minnesota wilderness area along the Canadian border probably has the highest loon density in the continental U.S. In 1984, one 11,000 acre sample of surface water in the Boundary Waters Wilderness Area gave biologists a look at 125 loons, a loon for every eighty-eight acres. At that density New Hampshire's Lake Winnipesaukee would have about 500 loons, instead of the forty-three loons it had in 1984.

Prospects:

Minnesota should continue to be the land of the loon for many more years. The state's non-game office has given considerable attention to loon management, and Minnesotans take loon protection very seriously. The population should remain at its present level, which is higher than the total of all the other U.S. states (excepting Alaska) combined.

Private Loon Organizations:

The annual survey is conducted by the Minnesota DNR, which also sponsors important research on chemical contamination of loons. A Twin Cities-based group, the Minnesota Loon Appreciation Committee, conducts public education programs.

North Dakota

Official State Classification: None

The common loon has been designated a Watch Species by the Endangered Species Committee of the North Dakota Chapter of The Wildlife Society.

Historical Perspective:

Records of loons in North Dakota date back to 1895.

Loon populations in North Dakota were probably never great and were restricted to the extreme northern areas.

Present Population:

According to Randy Kreil, Zoologist for The North Dakota Natural Heritage Inventory, loons are limited to the Turtle Mountain area in Bottineau and Rolette Counties near the Canadian border. While a population survey has not been conducted for loons, Kreil believes the population to be quite small. A 1972 book, *The Breeding Birds of North Dakota* by Robert Stewart, terms the common loon "fairly common" in the Turtle Mountain area and lists sixteen lakes in that area which support loons. All of these lakes are in woodland areas.

Prospects:

While there are no organizations concentrating on the loon, there is interest in the bird's future. A non-game check-off bill is under consideration by the state legislature which could provide funds for future research and management efforts.

Private Loon Organizations: None

Montana

Official State Classification: None

Historical Perspective:

Early naturalist's records indicate loons have been present in small numbers on remote Montana lakes.

Present Population:

A survey conducted in 1984 by Don Skaar under the auspices of the North American Loon Fund covered 186 lakes and located twenty-seven breeding pairs, and an additional nineteen pairs whose breeding status was unknown. The Montana population is estimated at, according to Skaar, a "conservative" 150 loons. Loons were found on lakes in wooded areas only, rather than on lakes in open grassland areas. Loons were not found on lakes at altitudes above 5,000 feet.

Prospects:

The loon population appears to be stable.

Private Loon Organizations: None

Pacific Northwest

Historical Perspective:

Officials in Washington, Oregon and California indicate that common loons once bred in small numbers in all three states. California's last documented loon nesting was in 1944 when pairs were sighted on three northern California lakes. Washington and Oregon had loons only into the first quarter of this century.

Present Population:

There are no confirmed nestings of common loons in any of the Pacific Northwest states, but Kelly McAllister of the Washington DNR Non-Game office thinks there may be loons in some remote areas of the state, and Harry Nehls, an Oregon birder, believes there could be a pair or two on Oregon's backcountry Cascade lakes. All three states have substantial numbers of wintering loons along their coastlines.

Prospects:

Based upon the comment of the states' non-game officials, it appears unlikely that populations of breeding loons will return to the Northwest.

Private Loon Organizations: None

Alaska

Official State Classification: None

Historical Perspective:

Loons of all four species have been common in Alaska. Unfortunately few records were kept. The frequent references to loons in Eskimo legends indicate loons have been part of Alaska's natural heritage for a long time.

Present Population:

Alaska has a lot of loons. Paul Arneson, the coordinator of the state's Non-Game Species Program, doesn't have any official population estimates but does have a strong feeling that there are no problems with the loon populations in Alaska.

There are unofficial population estimates for the state. For twenty years, James King of Juneau coordinated the U.S. Fish and Wildlife's duck and goose breeding surveys. For fifteen of those years, he counted loons as well. Based upon his 1983 data from 214 survey areas of the state, he can make "ballpark" estimates of the populations for three loon species. The numbers are impressive: arctic loon—212,000, common loon—34,000, and red-throated loon—22,000.

Breeding only in extreme northern Alaska, the yellow-billed loon was not included in King's survey work. The population of yellow-billed loons is much smaller than any of the other loon species, but its population appears stable. While not the most numerous of the loon species in Alaska, the red-throated loon is the most widely distributed in the state.

Prospects:

Dan Gibson of the University of Alaska Museum in Fairbanks believes loons are "doing well" and will continue to do well. Even the highly publicized North Slope oil developments probably will not affect population levels, according to Gibson, because these developments involve only a fraction of Alaska's coasts, a habitat loons use only casually anyway. With its tremendous populations of common, red-throated and arctic loons, Alaska is and will continue to be a mecca for loon lovers.

Private Loon Organizations: None

CANADA

Historical Perspective:

Common loons have been so plentiful for so long in so much of Canada that relatively little attention has been paid to them. Except for the southern plains areas of Alberta and Saskatchewan and the arctic regions of the far north, loons have been as common as crows in Canada.

Present Population:

Canada has a lot of water. Ontario alone has 250,000 lakes, making a loon census there an intimidating task. The Long Point Bird Observatory has started doing random sample lake surveys but no province-wide estimates are yet available. In well developed southern Ontario, loon numbers are modest, but from a line north of North Bay and Sault Ste. Marie loons are generally abundant. To the northwest, in the popular sport fishing areas around Kenora and Ignace, loons populate virtually every lake.

Peter Croskery, the Fish and Wildlife supervisor in Ontario's Ministry of Natural Resources Ignace office, has conducted common loon surveys in northwestern Ontario. He considers the loon population to be very healthy, even "in excess of its natural carrying capacity," in his end of the province. He views the large numbers of non-territorial loons on many Ontario lakes as evidence of a "surplus" stock, waiting to fill any available territory. Croskery cited, as a case in point, one lake of 6,000 acres which in 1984 had fifty breeding pairs and as many as seventy-five extra loons. He estimates the population in his district at about forty loons per 100 square miles, a figure he believes can be generalized to most of northwestern Ontario.

Prime loon habitat starts to fade, though, near Hudson Bay. The roughly 100,000 square miles of the Hudson Bay lowlands probably do not support as many loons as the areas around Ignace, according to Harry Lumsten, a wildlife researcher based in the Ministry's Maple office. One survey conducted to monitor goose populations turned up only fourteen loon nests over a 150-square-mile area. Considering the size of the Hudson Bay lowlands, that estimate would still convert to nearly 20,000 loons.

While wildlife officials are reluctant to attempt a province-wide estimate, it is clear the number of Ontario loons would dwarf the total U.S. common loon population.

Ontario's neighboring province of Quebec has about a million lakes and a fair number of loons. A government study in 1979 placed the province total at 70,000 common loons and 5,000 red-throated loons.

Saskatchewan is famed for its trophy fishing and wilderness lakes. While no official estimates of loon populations are available, Dale Hjertaas, Wildlife Ecologist for the province's Parks and Renewable Resources Department, notes there are 90,000 lakes in the northern part of Saskatchewan alone, and most lakes have at least two or three breeding pairs. Like Ontario, Saskatchewan is a loon paradise.

A bit further to the northwest and north the population of loons is also substantial. In addition to his Alaskan surveys, James King covered the Yukon Territory and the Northwest Territories while conducting duck and goose breeding surveys. Again he counted loons. While the Yukon had fairly sparse loon counts, the Northwest Territories were loaded. His rough estimates for the Yukon Territory were: arctic loon—1,500, common loon—500, and red-throated loon—1,200. For the Northwest Territories which sprawl across the top of Canada his estimates, based upon 240 survey transects were: arctic loon—175,000, common loon—137,000, and red-throated loon—34,000. Additional loon populations exist in Alberta, which has about 3,000 common loons according to officials there, and in British Columbia, New Brunswick and Newfoundland, but population estimates for those areas are not available.

A picture of loon abundance emerges when viewing the Canadian loon situation. While numerical estimates based upon a slim data base are always dangerous, they are also always interesting. If some new spy satellite could count Canadian loons, it would not be shocking to discover that maybe a half million loons swim in Canadian waters. It's a guess but an informed one, give or take 100,000.

Prospects:

Loon numbers might decline in the heavily populated areas of Canada. Since Canada's human population is concentrated in southern Quebec and southeast Ontario (south of a line from Quebec City to Sudbury), the nation's loon population still has vast areas of relatively undisturbed lake country. Acid rain is the major cloud on the loon's horizon. David Hussell, an Ontario biologist who conducted the Long Point Bird Observatory's loon project for several years, estimates seventy percent of Canada's loons live in areas sensitive to acid rain. When that problem is licked, Canadian loons should have fairly smooth sailing.

Common loon on nest in alert position.
PHOTO BY WOODY HAGGE

Making a Living

"I have laid aside business, and gone a-fishing."

—Izaak Walton, 1653

In 1919, Arthur Cleveland Bent, the serious scientist with the lively prose, deftly captured the fishing prowess of the common loon: "This loon feeds largely on fish, which it pursues beneath the surface with wonderful power and speed. The subaqueous rush of the formidable monster must cause consternation among the finny tribes."

The underwater hunting skills of loons obviously impressed Bent. Many sport fishermen were similarly impressed and probably wondered and worried about the diet of the loon. In his study of diving birds, Bent described the fisherman's worst nightmare: "Even the lively trout, noted for its quickness of movement, cannot escape the loon and large numbers of these desirable fish are destroyed to satisfy its hunger." Bent quickly noted, however, that loons and trout had co-existed for thousands of years before the arrival of modern fishermen. He was satisfied that it is not "fair to blame this bird, which is such an attractive feature of the wilds, for the scarcity of trout."

Many fishermen of Bent's era shot loons as competitors, and even pushed for bounties on loons, but Bent answered their charges with a comment remarkably sensitive for the time: "We are too apt to condemn a bird for what little damage it does in this way, without giving credit for the right to live." Bent was a man ahead of his times, but the slaughter of loons continued.

In today's more enlightened era, few loons are shot by selfish fishermen, but Bent was right about trout—loons do have a taste for them. Trout of considerable size apparently are fair game for common loons. In New York's Adirondack region, three common loons were found in trap nets. Analyses of the loons' stomachs by state biologists revealed the presence of metal tags which are routinely attached to stocked brook trout.

Since the size of the trout when tagged and the date of release were known, it was possible for officials to estimate the size of each trout when it met a loon for lunch. Some of the trout were estimated at eighteen inches—big brook trout by anyone's standard. An eighteen inch brook

Immature loon photographed in shallow pond at Northwoods Wildlife Center in Minocqua, Wisconsin. A real "fishing-machine." PHOTO BY BOB BALDWIN

trout would weigh nearly two pounds, not a bad meal for an eight pound loon. While no one actually saw these loons consume trout, it is unlikely the loons could have picked up the tags in any other way. A study from Michigan supports the New York evidence. A Michigan biologist, G. R. Alexander, analyzed the stomachs of a dozen loons. He concluded their diet consisted of eighty percent trout, ranging in size from six to twelve inches. Loons in Ontario's Algonquin Park also dine on trout. One common loon found there had tags from twenty-five trout in its stomach.

However, loons should not be characterized as aquatic gourmands, feasting only upon the finest gamefish. To the contrary, they are highly opportunistic aquatic hunters and will eat whatever is handy. If they live on trout lakes, they will eat trout, but most likely they will find other prey more abundant and easier to catch. Since more typical loon prey (such as sucker or perch) is rarely tagged, evidence of eating fish other than prime gamefish like trout is not readily available.

In many ways the loon/trout issue is like the wolf/deer debate. While wolves eat deer, they do not eat enough to threaten the deer population. In a similar fashion, loons are not serious competitors for the sport fisherman. Since they feed on almost anything that swims, loons take relatively few game fish. Some scientists, in fact, believe loons might actually improve sport fishing by removing large numbers of rough fish.

A Balanced Diet

Although loons do eat a lot of fish, they also sample a wide variety of other prey items. In his *Handbook of North American Birds*, Ralph S. Palmer estimates the common loon's diet at eighty percent fish. In fresh water these fish are typically perch, suckers, bullheads, sunfish, smelt, and various minnows. Some non-finned items like frogs, salamanders, crayfish and leeches are also on the loon's menu. An examination of one loon found dead on Squam Lake in New Hampshire turned up only a collection of crayfish in its stomach.

In his Master's thesis on loons, Sigurd Olson summarized the results of analyses of twenty-seven stomachs taken from loons throughout the upper midwest. The information revealed not just what loons ate, but also how they ate. Of the twenty-seven stomachs, twenty contained only one species of fish. Apparently when loons find a good thing they stick with it, feeding—at least for awhile—exclusively on that species. The most common prey items were yellow perch (ten loons), suckers (five), and minnows (three). Other prey found included black crappie (two), walleye (two), northern pike (one), black bass (one) and pumpkinseed sunfish (one).

The extent of the loon's adaptive feeding behavior is impressive. In a 1945 study of British Columbia lakes, J. A. Murno discovered some common loons living throughout the summer on lakes containing no fish. Yet, he saw healthy loons in breeding plumage. Upon inspection of the stomachs of four loons, Murno found only mollusks, amphipods (small invertebrates) and insects. Loons, especially chicks, can be vegetarian, eating a variety of aquatic greens. One juvenile loon found in Minnesota had a gizzard completely full of vegetable matter.

Less is known about the loon's salt water diet, but at a minimum herring, sea trout, rock cod, flounder and various crustaceans and mollusks are on the menu. As in freshwater, availability is probably a more important factor than flavor.

Whether loons are on salt or fresh water, they spend a lot of time fishing. They always capture live prey. In his many years on loon waters, Olson never observed a loon eating a dead fish. Once I tried to feed a pair of curious loons some dying and dead minnows. Even though the loons were only thirty feet from my canoe and were aware, I'm sure, of the minnows hitting the water, they didn't take the bait.

A "peering" loon. Loons fish by sight and usually spot their prey before they dive. PHOTO BY WOODY HAGGE

This six week old common loon is ready for its own fishing expeditions. PHOTO BY WOODY HAGGE

One member of the pair is diving for lunch while the other is casually preening. For loons, fishing is just a way to make a living. PHOTO BY WOODY HAGGE

When loons are not preening or resting, they are probably fishing or on their way to a fishing area. PHOTO BY WOODY HAGGE

Big Appetites

Mark Blackbourn, director of The Northwoods Wildlife Center in Minocqua, Wisconsin, has had a lot of experience with captive loons. In five years he has handled sixty injured loons and has returned fifty of them to northern Wisconsin lakes. Feeding loons while they recuperate from a variety of injuries has been a challenge for the clinic's staff. Blackbourn quickly learned that loons do not like to be fed, but need to capture their own minnows. To keep captive loons healthy and happy, Blackbourn constructed a small pond about twenty feet long and three feet deep. Keeping a loon in live minnows is no small task. A recovering loon typically would capture and eat eight dozen four-inch minnows per day, supplemented by a dozen or more crayfish. During daylight hours, the loons either fed or preened, with occasional naps on shore. (Contrary to conventional loon wisdom, Blackbourn has also observed non-nesting wild loons preening and sleeping on shore, even well after the nesting season.)

Blackbourn's report of loons eating a hundred minnows a day will not surprise research biologists. The loon's food requirement, at least during the nesting season, is enormous. Jack Barr, a biologist from the University of Guelph in Ontario, estimates that a pair of loons with two chicks will consume over a ton (2,310 pounds to be exact) of fish during the fifteen-week chick-rearing period.

There have been many reports of "greedy" loons. In 1927, a loon near Erie, Pennsylvania was found dead with a fifteen-inch pike-perch (walleye) in its throat. In a 1929 article, Edward Howe Forbush mentions loons on Nantucket Bay swallowing flounders five inches from belly to dorsal fin. Bent also saw flounder-loving loons, including one loon which had fifteen flounders averaging four inches in length in its gullet, in addition to a stomach nearly full of a partially digested fish. To handle such large prey, loons have developed a rather elastic esophagus. These are, how-

While loons can handle fairly large prey like this perch, they generally take smaller fish or minnows.   PHOTO BY DAVE REPP

ever, examples of unusually large prey and loons more typically feed often, but on small prey. According to Jack Barr, the average weight of prey is only three-quarters of an ounce.

No avian gluttons, loons just have to keep up with a high level of energy expenditure. For most birds, just maintaining their body temperature requires a large number of calories. Birds generally eat relatively more for their weight than do other animals. The golden eagle consumes over a pound of food a day—fifteen percent of its body weight. The pelican devours about four pounds of fish a day—half of its weight. Ever watch a hummingbird? They feed almost constantly and consume more than their body weight every day.

Fishing Techniques

Generally loons swallow their prey under water, but there are a few reports of loons coming to the surface with food. Olson once watched a loon on Como Lake, near St. Paul, capture small panfish and bring them to the surface to tear apart. Since the dorsal fin on sunfish is quite large and has extremely sharp points, loons would have a hard time swallowing such spiny prey.

Loons feed by sight alone and do not need cues of sound or odor, but do require relatively clear water to forage efficiently. Barr points out that as water clarity diminishes, loons start bottom feeding and fill up on slow-moving crayfish. Because of their sight-hunting methods, loons do not feed at night.

The loon's superb diving abilities and opportunistic tendencies have created problems for commercial fishermen on Lake Superior. Fishermen there use pond nets, large net enclosures with a lead or opening which funnels into the net. Since there is no cover over the net on the water's surface, Lake Superior's loons and cormorants quickly discovered that while fishing in the open lake may be good, fishing within these large pond nets is even better. While loons may not actually kill many trapped fish (most are too large), they do chase them into the sides of the net where many fish gill themselves in the net mesh and die. There is some spoilage which causes an economic as well as a time loss for commercial fishermen. Stories of fishermen carrying shotguns to deal directly with the problem are still common.

In 1950, Sigurd Olson interviewed ten commercial fishermen on the Minnesota side of Lake Superior. While all had caught loons on their setlines baited for trout, one fisherman claimed to have caught forty loons in one day on a 200 hook setline. Many fishermen thought the loons had "learned" to spot the setline floats. Understandably, these fishermen did not have a deep appreciation for loons.

PHOTO BY DAVE REPP

While most wanted a bounty on loons, their wish was never realized. The sea lamprey entered the big lake in the early 1950s and settled the issue by destroying nearly all the trout in Lake Superior. With no trout to catch, the fishermen didn't need to worry about a few loons in their setlines; they went out of business or changed their target species and their fishing techniques. Then in 1961 the common loon prevailed over such beautiful birds as the wood duck, the scarlet tanager and the belted kingfisher to become the Minnesota State Bird. The loon, as they say, had arrived.

Wilderness Music

"If perchance you have never had the good fortune to hear the mournful cry of the common loon, you have missed the full enjoyment of the wilderness. Like the howl of a timber wolf, the bugling of a bull elk and the singing of a humpback whale, the mournful cry of the loon is unique."

—*George Harrison, 1983*

More than unique, loon music is primitive, reaching into obscure recesses of the human mind. For some people, loon calls might reach down a little too deeply. A few years ago, a resort owner in northern Wisconsin told me the story of a Chicago couple who spent just one night in a lakeside cabin and checked out early the following morning. The loons just "got to them," he said. Apparently they felt more secure in the jungles of the Loop.

Getting to People

Loon vocalizations *get to* a lot of people. There is something about loon music that unleashes the poet in many people. Despite his lofty reputation as a philosopher, Henry David Thoreau was often a stiff, pedantic writer, producing endless paragraphs about the number of nails in his cabin. But when Thoreau writes about loons, he becomes a hopeless romantic. In *Walden*, he describes a loon's call:

"The loon uttered a long-drawn unearthly howl, prob-

ably more like that of a wolf than any bird; as when a beast puts his muzzle to the ground and deliberately howls. This was his looning, perhaps the wildest sound that is ever heard here, making the woods ring far and wide."

Thoreau's Walden Pond is quiet these days, except for the laughter from the popular swimming beach and the occasional squealing of car tires. It is not a place for loons or poets.

Writing in a 1924 National Audubon Society leaflet, Arthur Norton captured the spirit of the loon with poetic prose worthy of Byron or Shelly:

"The loon manifests uneasiness before a storm . . . maybe its savage spirit is stirred to depths of exultation by the turmoil of wind and wave for, with the rising gale, the bird becomes especially noisy, sending its powerful voice echoing across the water with great frequency. Like the spirits of old legends, it seems never to sleep, but to be ranging these realms both day and night, sending abroad wild, loud notes at all hours."

Is he talking about the serene loon swimming on your lake? A "savage spirit?" Is loon music then a key which unlocks hidden doors of the psyche? That would explain why even very proper birders such as Oliver Austin get a little carried away. In writing his authoritative *Birds of the World,* Austin was all business, except for two pages devoted to loons. There he found space for a personal tribute to loon music:

> "It embodies the very spirit of far places, of forest-clad lakes where the clear air is scented with balsam and fir . . . no one who has ever heard the diver's music, the mournful far-carrying call notes and the uninhibited, cacophonous, crazy laughter, can ever forget it."

Even in 1899 the call of the loon had not gone unnoticed. In his definition of loon for the *Century Dictionary,* William Whitney added an editorial note: "The wild actions of the loon in escaping danger and its dismal cry suggest the idea of insanity; hence the common American simile 'as crazy as a loon.' " Times certainly have changed: few today would term loon music "dismal."

Even fewer people try to forget the loon's extraordinary calls. Loons have entertained generations of lakeshore visitors and have inspired a measure of national pride. In his book *Birds of Ontario,* L. L. Snyder described loon calls in language brimming with nationalistic feeling: Loon calls are " . . . as characteristic of our northland as bold rocks and blue waters, and as effective in inducing Canadian nostalgia as the odor of evergreens, or the taste of blueberries."

The calls are arresting yet mysterious. Despite years of listening, Sigurd Olson believes loon calls remain the "least understood attribute of the loon." By varying slightly the four basic call types, he believes loons create an "almost endless repertoire" of wilderness music. That's the gospel according to Olson.

According to Framingham State College biologist William Barklow, however, loon calls can be understood. And if anyone can understand loon vocalizations, it's Barklow,

who has spent seven years studying and recording loon calls. Loon lovers should thank Barklow for his detailed doctoral dissertation, *The Functions of Variations in the Vocalizations of the Common Loon,* and the record album, *Voices of the Loon,* a superb collection of loon recordings published in 1980 by the North American Loon Fund and the National Audubon Society.

Not content with just listening to loon calls, Barklow literally disassembled them. Using high tech equipment, Barklow produced audiospectrographs, sort of acoustical fingerprints or voice prints of loon calls. Also known as sonograms, audiospectrographs are made when a stylus transfers frequency patterns to a moving belt of paper. With such a visual representation, loon calls can be analyzed with a discrimination far exceeding that of the human ear. These "images" of calls can also be fed into a computer for more detailed analysis and comparison with other loon calls.

While some people might worry about technology stealing some of the romance of loon music, they should recognize that these techniques allow scientists to hear more of the music and probe more deeply into loon communications. This research is giving loon devotees a deeper appreciation of the complexities of loon language without removing the magic.

Loon Language

Long before Bill Barklow carried his microphone into the backcountry of northern Maine, the four basic loon calls had been clearly identified. In his 1919 study of loons and other divers, Arthur Cleveland Bent quotes William Underwood's description of common loon calls:

> "First, a short, cooing note, often heard when there are several loons together; second, long drawn-out note, known among the guides as the night call; third, the laughing call, which is familiar to everybody who has ever been in loon country; and fourth, another call

which is not often heard, known among the guides as the storm call. The last is a very peculiar and weird performance which the guides regard as a sure sign of a coming storm."

Without the aid of any tape recorders or other listening devices, Underwood had described quite accurately the hoot, wail, tremolo and yodel. His comment about the yodel being a storm call has not, however, stood up well through the years. Neither the yodel nor any other loon call predicts the weather any better—or worse—than the evening news.

While loon language does rest upon these four basic parts of loon speech, it also embraces a few extra pieces of vocabulary. Often calls are accidently or deliberately (who knows?) combined to create additions to the loon lexicon. Fusions of the tremolo-wail and tremolo-yodel are frequently heard, delighting listeners and confounding researchers. Are these confused or clever loons? If the tremolo call implies a tendency to flee and the wail a need to establish contact, as several researchers suggest, does then the tremolo-wail reflect a deranged or even schizophrenic loon mind? Probably not. People change their minds, why not loons?

Further complicating loon linguistics are the frequent reports from many sober loon listeners of "different" calls. Even people who have memorized the *Voices of the Loon* album have heard loon calls which simply do not fit any call type or combination type. Give Barklow a few more years with his technological ears to settle the questions. In the meantime loon listeners can learn a lot by tuning in the four basic calls.

The Tremolo

Reacting to the common loon's tremolo call, writer John McPhee reflected, "If he were human, it would be the laugh of the deeply insane." It's probably this call which drove the Chicago tourists out of their lakeside cabin. But getting

Glenn Irwin's favorite loon, Maggie McGook, would sometimes give tremolo calls while on the nest.   PHOTO BY GLENN IRWIN

a tremolo call on paper is like catching a brook trout with bare hands—it may be fun to try but one should not expect much for dinner. Barklow called the tremolo "a relatively slow frequency modulation with a superimposed modulation of amplitude." Then he got technical. It's a good thing we have the *Voices of the Loon* album and the opportunity to hear many thousands of the real callers. To appreciate the tremolo or any other loon call you simply have to hear it.

While any motivational inferences about the tremolo are just informed guesses, Barklow and others have developed some well-supported theories. After several years of attempting to put loon calls and behaviors together, Barklow has defined the tremolo as the loon's all purpose call which can signal alarm, annoyance, worry or greeting. Isolating three different types of tremolos, Barklow suggests the tremolo could provide a graded sytem of communication between loons. The lower frequency calls reflect a low level of anxiety or intensity while the high frequency tremolo calls reflect a sense of urgency. Barklow has designated these simply Types 1, 2 and 3 with Type 1 being the lowest and Type 3 the highest level of intensity.

According to Barklow, the ability to modify the "meaning" of a single call is rare in birds or other animals. Apparently loons can send very different messages by increasing the duration and frequency of the tremolo. The longest and most complex of the tremolo calls, the Type 3 call, is usually reserved for occasions of extreme alarm or anxiety.

In Barklow's view, all three tremolo types usually signal a tendency to flee. Usually the tremolo is coupled with behavioral responses such as a dive, a run on the surface or a take-off. The presence of people often elicits the tremolo, especially when boaters or fishermen approach too closely. University of Stockholm scientists, Sverre Sjolander and Greta Agren, documented quite well this disturbance-tremolo association. From a distance they observed people encountering loons. In ninety-four consecutive human disturbance situations, loons gave a tremolo call; no other calls were heard.

But the tremolo isn't reserved just for human encroachment. Millions of years before *Homo sapiens* appeared, the tremolo call echoed across ancient lakes. Loons often use the tremolo to communicate while flying; in fact, the tremolo is the only call loons can give while in flight. Loons are selective in their use of the tremolo when flying over lakes; Barklow noticed that loons flying over loon-less lakes were usually silent. Keeping track of when flying loons used the tremolo, Barklow heard tremolos only one of nine times a loon flew over a loon-less lake, but twenty-two of twenty-four times a loon flew over a lake holding loons.

Other situations which provoke the tremolo include, according to Barklow, the return of a loon's mate, social activities such as group displays, and chorusing with other loons. Attempting to relate the various tremolo types with particular loon behaviors, Barklow discovered that the Type 2 or middle ground call is the most versatile, accounting for over half of all tremolo calls. With the help of audiospectrographs, Barklow could even see subtle differences within call types. Some Type 2 calls reflect greater or lesser intensity. A low frequency Type 2 call might mean "let's get out of here" while a high frequency Type 2 might mean "let's get out of here *now*." These variations within variations give more meaning to Sigurd Olson's comment about an endless repertoire.

The Wail

Oliver L. Austin called the wail of the common loon " . . . one of the loveliest sounds in nature." Often termed the night call, the wail is probably the favorite call of contemporary loon watchers. John McPhee, a devoted follower of loon religion, believes the wail call "authenticates the northern lakes." That's quite a compliment, considering the many other options such as eagles, wild rice, lake trout, silence and the howl of the wolf. Many people, Thoreau and Olson included, have mentioned the wail of the loon and the howl of the wolf in the same breath. In his 1939 book, *The Natural History of Birds of Eastern and Central North America*, Edward H. Forbush captured the similarity beautifully: "Often toward nightfall I have heard his storm call far out to windward against the black pall of an approaching tempest like the howl of a lone wolf coming down wind." It might work both ways. Loon calls are known to elicit the howls of wolves and coyotes. I know the wail can stop dogs in their tracks. Our two not-so-wild collies freeze and utter low growls whenever a wail call comes through our stereo speakers during playings of *Voices of the Loon*.

Watching loons give the wail, Olson noticed that the call was given with the bill almost closed, causing the throat to swell considerably. He even put the call on paper—"ahaa-

A loon seconds before giving a wail call. Note the enlarged throat.
PHOTO BY WOODY HAGGE

ooo-oooo'oooo-ooo-ahhh." (Maybe he *can* catch brook trout with his bare hands.)

Looking at audiospectrographs of wail calls, Barklow sees a call with a structure very similar to the tremolo call. He hears in the wail the most primitive loon sounds and notes that the wail is the first call attempted by chicks. On his audiospectrographs Barklow sees, as with tremolos, three distinct call types, going from simple to complex calls. The Type 1 is a relatively unchanging tone lasting usually just a couple of seconds. Types 2 and 3 last longer and include tonal jumps. Normally wails are given in a series of five to twenty calls.

The wail conveys a general message. While it is usually a signal for interaction, this call's exact function depends upon its context. Often the wail is used to re-establish contact with a mate; it is the call of choice when a loon on the nest wants to exchange places with its mate. Frequently the wail is used in night chorusing, often opening and closing the concert, and in answering the tremolo of loons flying overhead. Wails are used for contacting other loons and they work for contacting people as well, penetrating human consciousness to the deepest levels. What would our northern lakes be without this mournful cry of the wilderness?

The Yodel

Listening to the yodel call of the common loon is a twilight zone experience. Sigurd Olson describes it as "the weirdest and wildest of calls . . . beautiful and thrilling . . . maniacal and blood-curdling." He even spelled it for us— "a-a-whoo-queee'queee-wheoooo'-queee", but drew the line at trying to interpret the endless variations of the yodel. In 1950, Olson believed that task was impossible. In the 1980s, with modern equipment, researchers are trying. Because it can be used to identify individual loons, the yodel has opened new horizons in contemporary loon research. The audiospectrographs of a given loon's yodel calls give one-of-a-kind voice prints. After studying yodel audiospectrographs of the same loon from different years, Barklow is convinced that a loon's yodel does not change over time, which provides researchers with the acoustical equivalent of bird banding.

For a species as difficult to capture and tag as the loon, this capability represents a major breakthrough in loon research. Other birds with unique individual calls include the chickadee, the indigo bunting, the white-throated sparrow and the song sparrow. Whether loons can recognize other loons as individuals is uncertain, but such recognition could serve a potentially valuable purpose by reducing aggression between neighboring pairs.

The yodel is the only loon call claimed by a single sex; it's given only by the male. Once field researchers see a loon giving the yodel call, they then can look for subtle plumage or behavioral variations to give them some needed help in field identification of the sexes. Ed Miller, a professor from Governors State University near Chicago, has worked on loon vocalizations for many years in the Wisconsin-Michigan border country near the Sylvania wilderness area. Aided by his field experience, he can distinguish one male from another without the aid of any equipment, and like other scientists, is convinced that the yodel call is exclusive to the male.

The message of the yodel has been fairly well defined—it is the loon's territorial imperative. Barklow calls it the "attack" message which conveys an aggressive message to nearby birds. During territorial confrontations, the yodel is frequently used in what Barklow calls "counter-singing." Imagine two boys shouting across their parents' property lines and you've got the picture. When males are involved in this singing match, the female on the territory will often support her mate with wails and tremolos. Even after the battle for turf is over, the resident male will often continue to yodel for an hour or more. While the use of the yodel peaks in early June, corresponding with incubation, yodels are heard throughout the summer. The yodel is most predictable when an intruding loon approaches another loon's territory, stimulating yodels seventy- five percent of the time, according to Barklow.

Several field researchers have mentioned that one stimulus always seems to provoke a yodel—a small low-flying airplane. Doing vocalization studies in northern Wisconsin, Rob Denkhaus, a University of Stevens Point graduate student, and Jim Pierce, Coordinator of Wisconsin Project Loon Watch, were having trouble getting yodels, often waiting hours to record one. They found a solution when they went to the Ashland airport (not quite the size of O'-Hare) and recorded small planes taking off. Bingo. Yodel calls, and only yodel calls, responded to each playing of the airplane tape.

The yodel has considerable variability. Middle sections of the call can be repeated reflecting the intensity of the call and the strength of the stimulus. In his audiospectrographs, Barklow sees as many as eight of the middle units repeated, creating a call as long as six seconds. By contrast, the familiar call of the chickadee lasts only a second. He believes the longest yodels, and consequently the most heated loon discussions, occur during night chorusing.

Two other scientists have taken a close listen and look at the yodel. Lynda Rummel and Charles Goetzinger have studied common loons in Algonquin Provincial Park north of Toronto and on Press Lake in the Kenora District of Ontario. They view the yodel as a total audio-visual display in which the call is only half the show. The other half is a posture—the loon's hunching down low in the water with its neck and head horizontal to the water and the bill tipped up slightly. After giving the yodel call, loons bring their heads back to the alert position with the neck raised and head high. Rummel and Goetzinger's observations support Barklow's view of territorial connections. They often watched a defending loon begin a yodel exchange with the intruding bird. While yodeling, the defender faced the intruder directly with wings cocked and extended horizontally. Usually the confrontation ended quietly with the intruding bird casually swimming away. This territorial defense did not always extend to non-paired, single birds. Rummel and Goetzinger often watched unmated birds pass freely through territorial waters.

The yodel is also used to settle non-territorial disputes during summer flocking periods. While loons are social, they have their limits; the yodel is a handy signal to tell other loons to "back-off."

The Hoot

This one-note call sounds just like it reads if you go softly on the "t." Frequently used but not often reported because it is a quiet, intimate call, the hoot is used mainly between family members and may serve an "I'm O.K./are you O.K.?" function. Barklow terms the hoot a location call, letting the mate or chicks know the sender's whereabouts. It is often used by adults to bring the chicks in close for feeding.

Other conversational sounds from loons include what Judy McIntyre calls the "mew" call. This call comes close to the soft cry of a human baby and is primarily used to communicate with chicks. McIntyre has heard adults luring the newly hatched chicks off the nest with the call. I recall first hearing the sound in 1980 during a September canoe trip. While watching an undisturbed adult and two nearly full-grown young, I heard frequent cries, like a gull but softer.

Night Chorusing

The full loon repertoire can best be appreciated during night chorusing. Early in the summer season, mid-May to mid-June in most regions, loons talk a good part of the night, using mainly the tremolo but also the wail and yodel. Of the many moments of loon magic, these are special. On the first night of a trip in May of 1970, I camped with three friends at Saganaga Lake right on the Minnesota-Canadian border. The calling began at sunset and lasted well into the night, and it will stay with me a lifetime. On an island in the middle of this sprawling border lake, we were surrounded and we surrendered. Sigurd F. Olson, writer and wilderness philosopher, described in his book *The Singing Wilderness* an evening of night chorusing on Lac la Croix, a similar lake about thirty miles to the west of the site of our Saganaga symphony:

> "That night it was still, and in the moonlight the loons began as I had heard them before, first the wild, excited calling of a group of birds dashing across the water, then answers from other groups until the entire expanse of the lake was full of their music. We sat around until long after dark and listened, but instead of be-

The crouch position often assumed when the yodel call is given. Note the brown under-feathers. PHOTO BY WOODY HAGGE

coming quiet as the moon went high, the calling increased and there again was the wild harmony, the music that comes only once a year, when it is spring on Lac la Croix."

Sigurd T. Olson, Sig's oldest son, was probably with his father that night, although there were too many similar nights to know for sure. Years later, after his formal study of loons at the University of Minnesota, Sig Jr. offered a couple of generalizations regarding loon choruses: choruses are restricted to spring and early summer and dusk to dawn, and they include most loons in the area. Most likely the role of these extravagant audio-displays is linked to territoriality; Barklow has observed pairs of loons going to the middle of their territory before joining the choir, perhaps to stake out their aquatic turf.

Calling at night is natural for loons. While the rates aren't lower, the conditions are perfect for long distance communications. Judy McIntyre, a Syracuse University biologist, points out that during the day loons can use visual cues, wing flaps for instance, to communicate, but at night they have only calling to keep in touch. During a two year study of loons in the Minnesota-Ontario border country, Jim Titus heard the peak of evening chorusing occur between the third week of May and the first week of June. (An association with nesting and related territorial defense is probable.) Titus described in his doctoral thesis a typical evening chorus: the first call is usually a wail, followed quickly by tremolos and an occasional yodel with calls spreading to every nearby loon until an area for miles around was "permeated with an orchestration of loon sounds."

Titus believed loons throughout his entire sixty-four square mile study area participated in the same chorus. While no one knows for sure how far loon calls carry, Sjolander and Agren estimated that the yodel of the yellow-billed loon can be heard by people for up to five miles. But here we are concerned with the hearing ability of loons, a more complicated unknown. Whatever the listening range of evening chorusing, all loon watchers should make a late spring trip to high-density loon country, like Minnesota's Boundary Waters Wilderness Area, Ontario's Quetico or Algonquin Provincial Park. The traveler will be rewarded with music that will echo in memory for a lifetime.

A Time to Listen

It is difficult to believe that the loon's incredible range of sounds come from a simple organ, the syrinx, in the lower part of the windpipe. So much music, so much meaning. Is it all territorial instinct or could loons be calling, partly at least, to express joy? I've never counted calls during a frenzied evening chorus. Each loon must call hundreds, if not thousands, of times. Could each call have a biological function? Most scientists would answer "yes", "probably" or "we don't have adequate data."

A traditional Ojibwa, Delores Bainbridge, would answer the question with a definite "no." She hasn't studied loons, but she knows loons. When an undisturbed loon, for no apparent reason, holds forth with a half-dozen beautiful wails, she knows that the loon is talking not only to other loons, but also to every other animal, including human, willing to listen. Humans in particular should listen carefully. In 1939, Edward H. Forbush suggested the loon's call seemed " . . . wailing and sad as if he were bemoaning his exile from his forest lake." Little did Forbush know that about half of a century later, loons would be missing from many of his favorite eastern haunts. It's time to listen.

A family portrait: pair with week-old chick. Depending upon lighting, a loon's beak can appear fairly light or almost black.   PHOTO BY WOODY HAGGE

Loons Through the Seasons

Northward Bound

"To anyone who has spent a winter in the north and known the depths to which the snow can reach, known the weeks when the mercury stays below zero, the first hint of spring is a major event. You must live in the north to understand it. You cannot just come up for it as you might go to Florida for the sunshine and the surf. To appreciate it, you must wait for it a long time, hope and dream about it, and go through considerable enduring."

—Sigurd F. Olson, 1957

For people who spend their winters in the north, spring is a precious season. In March there are always days when the mercury creeps up to fifty or sixty causing the snow on the south-facing slopes to retreat in panic. But the next day often brings bitter winds, more snow, and disappointment to birds and people waiting for spring. Later many migratory birds may be lured north by April's promise, only to freeze or starve in a misplaced blizzard. Not loons. When they come north, winter can be safely forgotten.

Loons seem to know exactly when their northern nesting lakes open. Often they arrive on the very day of ice-out. What pushes them north at precisely the right time? Is there animal ESP working here? Some telepathy between loons and year-around avian residents—owls, perhaps—telling loons the lakes are cracking and soft, calling them northward? Most scientists call this amazing timing "instinct," but that only names a fascinating mystery.

The Mysteries of Migration

Most birds participate in this mystery. Of the 215 species nesting in Michigan, for example, only twenty including grouse, quail, owls and woodpeckers accept winter's full challenge. In Canada and the northern United States, about two-thirds of all species here in the summer are gone in the winter. The spectacular migratory flights of ducks, geese and other waterfowl are seasonal milestones. For most waterfowl the journey is relatively short, often a thousand miles or less. For other birds a thousand miles is just a small step in the journey. The tiny barn swallow flies from Argentina to the Yukon and the globetrotting arctic tern makes a one-way trip of 11,000 miles every spring and fall.

A comprehensive understanding of the migration of birds has stubbornly eluded even the most sophisticated and persistent efforts of scientists. In some ornithological laboratory, scientists are probably debating right now the various theories of bird migration. There is no shortage of theories.

One theory postulates a system of orientation by the sun, giving birds the equivalent of a built-in solar compass. But many birds, including loons, often fly at night. Well, then, how about the theory that birds orient themselves by the stars? In the late 1940s, German ornithologist Gustav Kramer discovered that starlings in cages properly oriented themselves on clear nights but were totally disorganized on cloudy nights. Using a planetarium as a laboratory, Kramer's colleagues later refined this navigation-by-the-stars theory.

Studying migration at night has always been tricky. For years the best a birder could do was to watch for silhouettes across the face of the moon or send a powerful beam of light into the sky. Those techniques provided limited information. After World War II, a new era in migration studies unfolded—radar ornithology. Although designed for finding enemy aircraft, radar also found birds, and uncovered a wealth of information: night migration peaks at midnight and gradually falls off until dawn; night fliers apparently fly low, around 3,000 feet, and ignore ground features such as rivers, lakes or valleys, but still fly in a straight path.

Working out of Point Reyes Bird Observatory in California, Kenneth Able modified some Korean War vintage tracking radar, giving him the ability to follow individual birds over a wide flight path. On clear nights, he "watched" birds orient themselves in predictable migratory directions, but on nights with thick cloud cover he saw migrating birds fly with the wind even if it pushed them off their traditional migratory pathways. So the stars probably do play a role, but so does the wind.

The earth's magnetic field might also be involved. This theory emerged in 1855 and still claims followers. Experiments at Cornell University in the late 1960s revealed that pigeons with magnets on their backs were unable to find their home lofts and scattered at random when released. Pigeons with identical but non-magnetized bars on their backs returned directly to their lofts. This theory covers the successful migratory flights in dense fog or heavy rains where neither sun, stars nor wind could be involved.

It is safe to conclude that no single orientation system guides birds. Many cues are employed, possibly involving interplay among several orientation systems. The migratory debate will probably continue for many loon lifetimes, keeping migration a mystery beyond the reach of science.

While little is known about the "how" of migration, even less is known about the "why." If birds like it so well in South America, Mexico, or off the warm United States coastal waters, why don't they just stay there? They don't make trips of a thousand or more miles just to please northern tourists. Again, lots of theories. It is likely that the ice age pushed birds from their original northern breeding areas. When the glaciers receded some 20,000 years ago, descendants started returning to their ancestral homes. This approach, however, does not explain migration patterns in tropical areas. Competition provides a more general answer to the question of why birds don't live in the lands of perpetual sunshine. In tropical areas, bird densities are high. Birds of all description are forced to compete for the available food resource. Even in paradise only so many birds can be fed. In the broad northern temperate regions, competition is less severe. During the critical nesting and chick rearing period, birds in less crowded northern climes can find plenty of food and much more room.

Heading North

For loons in particular, the trip north in spring makes a lot of sense. There are far fewer stresses and dangers on the northern nesting lakes than on the coastal waters. Disease, pollution and violent storms are not as devastating in northern Minnesota or Maine as they are off the Florida coast. In fact, loon mortality on the summer nesting range is minimal. Of Wisconsin's roughly 3,000 loons, only five or six dead loons are found each summer.

Recent studies indicate that East coast loons start moving northward while still on Atlantic coastal waters and gradually work their way up the coast prior to overland migration to the breeding areas. While large numbers of loons winter off Florida's Atlantic coast, these loons leave by the first of April.

While movements of loons on the West coast are not as well studied, it appears a similar pattern of gradual migration is at work. Large numbers of loons, mainly arctic, start leaving southern California coastal waters in March. Guy McCashie, California editor for *American Birds*, talks to birders who see "tens of thousands" of loons pass some coastal points within a given week in early spring. Between March and May of 1977, one observer at Goleta Point just north of Santa Barbara counted 22,768 arctic loons, 4,355 red-throated loons and 3,891 common loons in just sixty-eight hours of observation. This river of loons, which probably winter in Mexican coastal waters, will not reach their probable Alaskan breeding areas until late May or early June.

Most lakes in loon country open in mid-to-late April, but in Alaska, and most of Canada, ice cover on the larger lakes is not unusual during the first week of May.

In 1950, Sigurd Olson identified an overland, "drifting northward," migratory behavior in loons that remains well accepted today. Common loons do not take off from the Florida coast in March and fly directly to Ontario, Michigan, Maine or any other nesting area. As ice recedes, they follow any open water, stopping to fish and rest, moving slowly northward. How else could loons hit the ice-out dates so accurately?

Olson also discovered that open lakes in central Minnesota held loons several weeks prior to the opening of the far northern lakes. In April and the first week of May in

Arctic loon in flight. Like common loons, arctic loons hold legs straight back.
PHOTO BY MARK PECK

1950, about twenty-five loons were present on Como Lake, right in the Minneapolis metro area. By May 6 all were gone. Centerville Lake, another early opening Minnesota lake just north of Minneapolis, had about 300 loons in late April but none after May 6. Similar reports have come from other northern states. In 1977, Gary Zimmer, a Wisconsin Department of Natural Resources loon researcher, observed sixty loons in early spring on the Wisconsin River, always an early opening river. They stayed for three days before moving on.

Loon Scouts

Perhaps loons utilize a "scouting" system with some birds traveling to the north, checking out the conditions and reporting back. The New Hampshire Loon Preservation Committee office has received numerous reports of loon tremolos heard in early spring when local lakes are still frozen. "I believe they're flying overhead," explains Committee director Jeff Fair, "perhaps on reconnaisance flights, checking for open water. I've seen them flying myself." While the scouting theory is speculative, it would provide loons with a mechanism for their otherwise uncanny ability to land on northern lakes often within hours of ice-out. When Sigurd Olson paddled into Knife Lake, a large wilderness lake in the Quetico-Superior Canoe Country, just two days after ice-out, he found loons waiting for him.

For loons, capable of flying over 90 mph, distance is not a major obstacle. At that speed a loon could travel from a "base camp" in the open waters of the southern Midwest to the northern nesting lakes in just a few hours. These flight speeds are impressive. Ducks and geese, by contrast, migrate at only 45 to 60 mph. Loons do hurry the spring migration. But then, they have to. Their early arrival to northern lakes is likely related to the brevity of the summer season. To secure a territory, find a nest site, lay and incubate eggs, care for chicks and get the juveniles flying before ice sets, the adults have few days to waste. The loons' arrival is probably geared to the ice conditions, not the calendar. If lakes open early, loons will usually arrive early.

That proposition holds up well in most, but not all, of loon country. It seems some of New Hampshire's loons are a bit tardy. As a former director of the New Hampshire Loon Preservation Committee, Scott Sutcliffe kept close track of spring arrivals. Loons there returned an average of nine days after the ice left New Hampshire's scenic lakes. Sutcliffe believes the short distance from New Hampshire's lakes to ice-free, oceanic wintering areas could be a factor in the late arrival.

Migratory Routes

The migratory routes of loons do not parallel the "regular" waterfowl routes. For mid-continent loons, there is not, for example, a Mississippi or an Eastern loon flyway. Rather, according to Judy McIntyre, there are multiple land routes. She notes that some Minnesota loons arrive via the Mississippi, while others cross into the state from Wisconsin, and still others fly up the center of the state. Loons heading north of the Great Lakes migrate in a general northwesterly direction.

McIntyre does see some evidence, though, for two distinct eastern North American breeding populations, one wintering on the Atlantic and the other on the Gulf coast. The Atlantic coast loons would gradually move north up the eastern seaboard until April when the birds would move overland to northeastern states, like New Hampshire, Vermont, New York and Maine, and to Quebec and northeastern Ontario. The Gulf coast loons would begin migrating in March and fly to Minnesota, North Dakota and possibly Wisconsin or the central Canadian provinces. While more research is required to support this hypothesis, it does offer an interesting framework for studying migration patterns. For West coast loons, the flight up the coast to Alaska is probably quite direct.

Welcome to Paradise

The eastern end of Lake Superior is an ideal place to study migrating common loons. Imagine seeing a thousand common loons in a single day. Volunteers at the Whitefish Point Bird Observatory in Michigan's Upper Peninsula don't have to: they counted 1,882 loons on May 8, 1982. In the peak hour of 8:00-9:00 a.m., volunteers recorded 740 flying loons. One hour. According to David Ewert, coordinator of the annual count, 4,838 loons were observed at the site between April 23 and June 6 with seventy percent of the total sighted during the four-day period of May 7 to 10.

Whitefish Bay on the "big lake" is a natural loon funnel. Nearly all of these loons are northbound birds. Before passing Whitefish Point, these loons may leave favorable feeding and resting areas in northern Lake Michigan or Huron. Departures of loons from these areas an hour or two after sunrise would account for the heavy flow over Whitefish Point in the 6:00-10:00 a.m. time period. Research is continuing at Whitefish Point to pinpoint the migration pathways.

The work of Ewert and other volunteers has generated some valuable migration data. While most loon observers refer vaguely to loons migrating alone or in small groups, Ewert gives specific information. Of 180 random observations of passing loons, the Whitefish Point volunteers recorded 104 individual birds, thirty-seven groups of two, twenty groups of three, ten groups of four, five groups of six, and four groups of between eight and eleven loons. The mean size of migrating groups was 1.91. Counting gets tough, Ewert recalls, on those days in May when loons pass in an "almost continuous stream."

Looking at a number of possible weather variables, Ewert found no strong relationships between wind direction or speed, cloud cover, temperature or barometric pressure and loon migration patterns. In contrast to other published reports, he did see loons flying against strong headwinds. Heavy rain or fog, however, apparently puts loons down. The Whitefish Point volunteers saw little or no migration activity during periods of heavy rain or dense fog. During light rain or moderate fog, loons appeared to fly at lower heights than during clear weather conditions. Loons generally fly higher over land than water. At inland sites in New York, Paul Kerlinger located loons by radar at altitudes of 7,000 feet, their ascent presumably aided by thermal currents.

Even for permanent residents of loon country, seeing a thousand loons is probably the work and pleasure of a lifetime. Seeing a thousand loons in a single day would be the experience of a lifetime for many. Pull out your Rand McNally and find Whitefish Point. It's just a bit north of Paradise, Michigan. Check your map. Dave can use a little more help.

Aquatic Turf

"The remote, spruce-edged lake shown under the cold, bright moonlit spring night; a gray crust, the last remains of winter's ice, glittered along the lake's shore. Abruptly the silence was broken by loud wails, yodels, eerie cries and splashing of water. It was our first signal that the loons had arrived back from their winter sojourn in the south, ready for another season."

—David Ewert, 1983

Announcing their arrival on the northern lakes with yodel calls, common loons waste little time in establishing their territory. Most scientists believe the male (only the male gives the yodel call) arrives first, a few days to a week before the female. If a loon has a few breeding seasons behind it, the search for territory might be a short one. Although scientific evidence to support the view is slim, loons probably return to the same territory each year. In 1973, on the waters of Minnesota's Roseau Wildlife Area, Judy McIntyre captured an adult loon which she had banded in the same area the summer before. Of course, thousands of loon watchers see *their* loons return to *their* lake each year. Without some visual marker on the bird, however, those observations reflect more romance than reality.

The Pair-Bond

After establishing a territory, the male waits for the arrival of a potential mate. Recent findings suggest that the nest site itself is the magnet which brings individual loons together. If the pair-bonding alone between loons were strong enough to insure the annual spring reunion, it should also be strong enough to keep loons together on the fall migration and coastal wintering range, but it doesn't. Loons generally do not migrate as mated pairs, nor do they spend the winter together. When he was director of the New Hampshire Loon Preservation Committee, Scott Sutcliffe noticed that loon pair-bonds gradually disintegrated as the season progressed. By the time the birds congregated in fall, he noticed little typical pair behavior. These are strong arguments for the breeding-site-affinity argument. So perhaps it's not each other they love; maybe it's home sweet home.

With birds there are no firm rules about the duration of the pair-bonds. For grouse, the attachment lasts about as long as copulation—a couple of minutes. The ruby-throated hummingbird's family ties last only a few days. For the majority of perching birds, however, togetherness extends through the breeding season. Many large birds such

Loon ignores photographer and swims into dramatic close-up. Note the slight "over-bite" of the upper mandible.   PHOTO BY WOODY HAGGE as swans, geese and cranes mate for life. While most pair-for-life birds find another mate if the first mate dies, some are known to wait several seasons before mating again.

The bonds between birds can be strong. In 1901, W. H. Hudson, an English writer and naturalist, observed a female goose with a broken wing walking in the direction she should have been flying. Another goose, presumably the mate, was flying overhead, returning often to keep in contact. Together they moved southward on a doomed but touching expedition.

There would be significant biological advantages (particularly the familiarity with a territory and its food supply) if loons did return to the same nest site each year. After all, fishermen always return to familiar waters. To test the theory, Paul Strong, a biologist at the University of Maine in Orono, placed barricades in front of "traditional" nest sites

Loon in early spring surveys its territory.   PHOTO BY WOODY HAGGE

to make access to the sites quite difficult. He discovered that some loons, when they arrived later that spring, actually nested adjacent to his barricades. While he could not be certain that these loons nested on the sites in previous years, he could conclude that they demonstrated an unusual preference for a particular site. While Strong, a careful scientist, limited his conclusions, others might agree his experiment adds strength to the argument that loons do return to the same territory each spring.

Evidence also exists for the theory that a site which looks good to one loon will look as good to a different loon. Judy McIntyre watched two pairs of loons prove this point. After the nesting season, both members of one pair were killed. The following spring another pair of loons nested on the exact site used the year before. Lakeshore residents, unaware of the death of the previous year's pair, probably thought "their" loons had returned again. Look-alike loons can easily create confusion.

What does look good to loons? What is happening in the central nervous system of a loon coming north for the first time? Since two or three years of living on coastal waters would cloud any "memories" it might have of its natal home, the loon would know nothing about selecting nesting sites. The flying loon is armed only with instinct—a powerful, if mysterious ally which "tells" a loon that three things are needed to make a productive territory: an adequate food resource with water clear enough for foraging; a protected nest site close to water; and a place nearby to rear chicks, preferably a shallow bay sheltered from the wind.

Territory Size

Loon territories vary greatly in size. In northern Minnesota, Sigurd Olson identified territories ranging in size from small bays of fifteen acres to entire lakes of a hundred acres or more. On very large lakes, territories were defined by natural boundaries such as islands or long points. The first judgment call for a young male returning north and sizing up potential territories is a simple one of size—is the lake big enough? Although it's unusual, there are records of loons successfully nesting on lakes of ten acres. There is even a confirmed 1984 report of a pair successfully nesting on a northern Wisconsin lake of only 1.3 acres. So the old claim that loons need a quarter of a mile of wet runway just doesn't hold water.

Just how much water a loon pair requires depends upon many variables including the quantity of available prey. For field scientists, estimating territory size can be tricky. If there are several pairs of loons on a large lake, a researcher is tempted to simply divide the number of territorial pairs into the lake's total acreage. That number reveals the space available to each pair but does not give true territory size. For example, on New Hampshire's larger loon lakes, each territorial pair has about 475 acres to roam, while in northern Minnesota each pair has 72 acres. A study by K. S. Younge indicated that each loon pair in east-central Saskatchewan has only 43 acres of available space. The territories of New Hampshire loons are not really ten times larger than those of Saskatchewan birds. There is simply more water in between territories, empty space available for loons that just aren't there. In the high loon density areas of Minnesota and Saskatchewan, it is evident that loon territories cannot be larger than an average of 72 and 43 acres respectively, assuming territories do not overlap. Also, some room has to be allowed for the unmated loons on the lake. So don't ever expect loons to be as abundant as robins, which require only about one-half acre to sustain a family. By the same token we can expect to see more loons than bald eagles, which require nearly 2,000 acres of territory, or golden eagles, which need ten times that space.

What Kind of Lake?

Just any lake is not good enough for loons. They need more than water to survive, yet pinning down the critical factors in loon habitat is difficult. Loons live on shallow lakes with emergent vegetation, on deep lakes with no vegetation, on lakes with many islands, on lakes with no islands, even on lakes with no fish at all. The popular view of loons as creatures only of cold, deep-water lakes in the heart of the wilderness just doesn't fit the facts. Defying that stereotype, loons nest right on the edge of metropolitan Minneapolis, in central Massachusetts on the Quabbin Reservoir and in southern Michigan right down to the Indiana border, all unlikely places for this symbol of wilderness.

Ironically some of the likely places—the big, deep, clear and cold lakes of the far north—have limitations. Many of these lakes have short, simple food chains; so while they often have large fish, they often do not have many fish. The productivity and diversity of many northern wilderness

Note the dark plumage under the wings. Most artists depict the under-wing area as all white.   PHOTO BY WOODY HAGGE

lakes is actually considerably less than that of the typical shallow, warm-water lakes on the southern edge of loon country. While this does not render these large lakes loonless, it does imply that loons on these lakes will have large territories.

An ideal loon lake would have clear water and many small fish. But loons are pragmatic and often live on less than ideal lakes. Being flexible in their feeding habits, loons can utilize a broad range of lakes. Even quite shallow lakes with no game fish at all can support loons if there is an ample supply of minnows. In addition to being more productive, shallow lakes allow the loons' prey less room to roam, making escape from a fast-swimming loon a low-odds proposition. Clear water is critical for sight feeders and without it, loons are forced to feed off the bottom, which supplies a less than ideal diet. The loss of clear water, due to human settlement and the subsequent agricultural activities of the nineteenth century, may have been a major factor in this species' retreat to the northern end of its original breeding range.

It's My Lake

Territoriality is basic. Nearly all higher animals establish and defend their turf, be it wet, dry or a piece of sky. Probably every bicyclist or runner has encountered the farm dog who owned not just the farmer's yard but also part of the public road. Walk down any rural roadway during the nesting season for blackbirds or grackles and you will start to understand the notion of territory. During July in northern Wisconsin, I've had to forfeit the right-of-way more than once to swooping blackbirds. Blackbirds rarely attack humans, but Alfred Hitchcock had to get his inspiration for *The Birds*, his classic horror film, from somewhere.

While it is unlikely that any future Hitchcocks will produce a film showing flocks of loons terrorizing Meredith, New Hampshire or Ely, Minnesota, the defensive instincts of loons are quite evident; they don't enjoy the company of other waterfowl, especially during the nesting season. There are many reports of common loons attacking mallards that come a little too close, including one from biologist Jim Titus who on three occasions in northern Minnesota watched loons chase merganser hens with broods. In New Hampshire, Tudor Richards, a former Executive Director of the New Hampshire Audubon Society, observed an immature common loon attack four white-winged scoters. The loon "stalked" the scoters with a slow, low-profile approach, then made an underwater rush. There were no injuries except perhaps to avian pride.

A dramatic account of a loon attacking another bird was reported in the ornithological journal *Auk*. According to Jones and Obbard, an arctic loon approached the nest of a Canada goose. As the gander moved out to meet the intruder, the loon savagely attacked the larger bird. After thirty seconds of "violent splashing and flapping of wings," the goose retreated toward its nest but died en route. An examination of the goose revealed that the loon's bill had penetrated full length puncturing the goose's lung.

Reports of "killer loons" roaming Squam Lake surfaced during the 1984 New Hampshire Loon Festival. Several loon watchers on the lake are convinced a group of unmated loons—"the gang of ten"—attacked and killed two loon chicks. After working so hard to protect loons from people, the volunteers on Squam Lake were perplexed by the prospects of protecting loons from other loons.

This aggressive loon behavior should be put into perspective. While it happens, it is not common. According to the New Hampshire Loon Preservation Committee officials, the gang of ten's behavior resulted from the crowding of loons, possibly caused by unusual weather patterns. While loons encounter countless thousands of other birds without violent attacks, they can be tricked into aggressive behavior. In the summer of 1980, Rick Newton, a Wisconsin Project Loon Watch staff member, attempted to capture and band loons. To lure loons near the capture area, he placed a simple wood loon decoy near a nest site and then played recorded loon calls. It drove one resident loon over the edge. The loon swam directly to the decoy and began a fierce attack which left the soft pine decoy a little the worse for wear. No loons were banded that day but the intensity of territorial defense was dramatically demonstrated.

Physical battles between loons are rare. Studying loon territorial defense in Ontario's Algonquin Provincial Park, Lynda Rummel and Charles Goetzinger observed fifty-four confrontations between loons. Only two culminated in fighting or chasing and typically the territorial defense was only posturing or bluffing, a technique animals of the same species have been using for millions of years to avoid dangerous battles. If natural selection does move animals toward survival, not as individuals, but as a species, nothing would be gained if one loon killed or seriously injured another. Instead, loons will put on a good show, calling, threatening and intimidating.

This behavior is well-developed in many animals. Monkeys and wolves, for instance, have vicious-sounding encounters, which usually end quietly when the individuals or groups retreat. While describing the dramatic territorial defense of the howling monkey, writer Robert Ardrey, in his book *African Genesis*, captured this behavior superbly:

> "When two groups sight each other, each on the fringe of its territory, all break into total rage. Males, females, juveniles and infants become ants on a hot plate, leaping through the branches, scudding through the treetops, screeching, barking, chattering in frenzy. For thirty minutes rage has its way; then both sides retire from the field of glory. Losses have been nil; territory has been held inviolate; anger has been magnificent and satisfaction for both sides a maximum."

While loons do not rival the howling monkey in intensity of display, they employ a similar behavioral system—protection of territory without direct, physical contact.

The loon's ritual defensive behavior is the yodel/crouch, a combination of sound and sight designed to drive away trespassers. When confronted, a loon will raise its head, thrust its body forward, cock its wings and give the yodel call, the basic hostile message. Rummel and Goetzinger have compared this posture to the threat stance of the vulture, an unlikely comparison given our human perceptions of bird beauty, but nevertheless a descriptive one.

Although the vulture position of the common loon is used primarily for territorial defense of the nest area, it has also been observed during the mid-to-late summer social flockings. In these post-breeding flocks, loons apparently still like some privacy and use this display as a signal to "back off." A behavior exclusive to large lakes, this flocking occurs in a neutral zone between established territories. In these buffer areas large groups of loons often mingle peacefully with only occasional defensive posturing. On Knife Lake in northern Minnesota, Sigurd Olson identified a social area about the size of the three adjacent loon territories, where unpaired loons could wander at will. The territory of a nesting pair, though, is rarely left unguarded. In twenty-nine visits to established territories, Olson found loons on the territory twenty-three times.

Generally the intensity and frequency of the territorial defense increases toward the end of the incubation period and climaxes with the hatching of the chicks. Additional variables are the number and size of other territories on the lake. Studying loons in northern Minnesota, Jim Titus observed territorial defense far more often on large lakes which had many pairs of loons. On small lakes he often heard resident loons use yodel and tremolo calls to warn potential intruders flying overhead that "this lake is taken."

Titus did see evidence of nesting loons tolerating an intruding single loon, especially if the entry were some distance from the nest site. If these intruders were young, non-breeding loons, as he speculated, they would pose no threat to the nesting pair's territory. However, a mated pair of intruders is a different story, and a potential problem arises when recreational disturbance pushes loons into the hostile territory of nesting loons. While defending their nest site, disturbed loons cannot give adequate attention to incubating their eggs or brooding their chicks.

In his spectacular study area around Millinocket Lake in northern Maine, Paul Strong watched loons of a different stripe. The traditional view of territorial defense just doesn't fit these Maine loons. Several thousand hours of observations by Strong produced few sightings of territorial defense displays. Even during incubation and chick rearing periods, Strong often watched several loons casually wander into another loon's territory. Instead of chasing away the intruders, the resident birds just socialized. Strong's problem was often not knowing who was who—the resident and intruding loons behaved in exactly the same fashion. He also saw flocking behavior very early in the season; flocks which sometimes included one or both members of a nearby nesting pair. These observations over several seasons underscore the danger of stereotyping loon or other wildlife behavior.

Ray Anderson, a wildlife biologist from the University of Wisconsin-Stevens Point, observed similar non-aggressive behavior while conducting telemetry studies in 1984. He was watching a resident pair (one had a radio transmitter attached to its back, so later identification was definite) with two chicks when a group of four adults swam into the area. The resident loons "stashed" the chicks by escorting them to the shoreline but then proceeded to quietly socialize with the intruders. No defensive displays were given. In fact, there was no behavior to indicate nervousness or stress. Could these loons have been related, even offspring of the pair with the chicks? Impossible to say at this point. There is a possibility that something cues loons to defend sometimes but not other times.

Courtship

Like the territorial defense display, the courtship behavior of loons is ritualized. In most animals, specific behaviors of the opposite sex are needed to move things along;

This pair is cruising the shoreline probably looking for a nest site.
PHOTO BY GLENN IRWIN

the system's signs and signals must be exactly right to prevent breeding attempts between different species. With loons, however, all the evidence isn't in yet. While most scientists are convinced that the wild, frantic displays reported by many canoeists and fishermen are not courtship behaviors, they often disagree on just what is and what isn't courtship behavior.

Even though descriptions of courtship and copulation are rare, scientific literature does provide some insight. Writing in the ornithological journal *Auk* in January of 1970, Jean and James Tate from Cornell University described the courtship of a pair of loons on French Farm Lake in Michigan. They saw no dramatic displays, no overwater chasing, no aerial displays and heard no vocalizations. What they did see they termed "ritualized preening," with the loons often showing their throat patches. They observed bill dipping, head rubbing, tossing up of the head, and simultaneous dives. At times the pair, to the Tates, appeared to dive in perfect synchronization. Copulation occurred on land. The Tates summarized the courtship process as "secretive behavior and unobtrusive displays."

In her doctoral dissertation, Judy McIntyre describes common loon courtship as "simple, aquatic and diurnal." Like the Tates, she reports no overwater chases or aerial displays. In her view, the running and flight displays signal aggression, which could not strengthen the pair bond, and are probably territorial.

McIntyre believes the courtship process involves a combination of displays, including short dives, bill dipping, bill flicking (an abbreviated bill dip), tucking the head low and facing away (an appeasement gesture). She contends that both sexes use the same display while quietly swimming near the shoreline, often giving the soft "mew" vocalization. She believes diving plays a major role in courtship. Both a short, quiet dive and the splash dive were used in most of the courtship sequences she observed.

McIntyre observed copulation on terra firma only,

twelve times, involving four different pairs. Her observations divided about evenly into two separate procedures—male on shore first and female on shore first. When the male was on shore first, he attracted the female with the soft "mew" call, keeping his head low. If the female then approached, he slid off the site and waited until the female arrived on shore. With the female on land, he returned to the site and mounted her. Usually, after copulation, the female stayed on the site, sometimes beginning the first phases of nest building. If the female went to shore first, the process was speeded up. The male followed and mounted immediately. In this sequence nest building activities followed. Post-copulatory displays were not observed.

Sverre Sjolander and Greta Agren observed similar courtship behaviors between yellow-billed loons. They saw shoreline search-swimming but no elaborate courtship and twice they watched the female go ashore with the male following quickly. Copulation required only ten seconds after which the male returned immediately to the water. The female stayed on shore for about three minutes.

In the Crex Meadows area of northwestern Wisconsin, at least one pair of common loons did create a little fuss. William Southern observed two loons skimming over the water at varying speeds, striking the surface with their wings, one bird pursuing the other. Southern watched the pursuer overtake and mount the other loon, submerge for about forty seconds and resurface still coupled.

Unfortunately, some scientists cannot accept the possibility that loons might have a range of courtship behaviors. As with many other aspects of loon study, it's dangerous to say "always." While some animals do exhibit rigid, stimulus-response patterns, loons quite simply do not. After years of relative obscurity, loon behaviors are today being observed by thousands of interested people. Someone is bound to see something "new." No one should be disappointed.

Calling It Home

*"In breeding season loons love the solitude of northern lakes where shores are shaded
by fir and spruce and where the still pure water seldom mirrors a human face."*
—Edward H. Forbush, 1939

Loons are homebodies. It's one of the things people like best about loons: they can count on seeing their loon in their bay. While loons summer within a restricted territory of perhaps a hundred acres or less, they have for about six weeks in late spring an even sharper focus—the nest site. Except for occasional fishing trips by the non-incubating member of the pair, life during the nesting season revolves around a very small piece of ground and water.

The Nest Site

It's not difficult to find loon nests if one starts looking on islands. Of fifty-four nests in one Minnesota study area, fifty were on islands. Similar island preference has been documented in both New Hampshire and Alaska, where seventy percent of all loon nests were found on islands. Loon islands are usually small and have low-lying vegetation and generally loons select the side of the island protected from the prevailing winds.

The common denominator in nest site selection is proximity to water. Nearly all loon nests are right on the shore's edge. In New Hampshire, Scott Sutcliffe estimated the average distance from nest to lake at sixteen inches. Exactly how far the nest is from water varies, unfortunately, with the lake's water level. A loon pair might start the incubation period with their nest a convenient six inches from water but find their site landlocked if the lake level drops, or flooded if the level rises. One New Hampshire loon pair found their nest eighty-eight feet from water after the lake level dropped. Traveling that distance over land or mud is no small task for birds so poorly adapted for locomotion on land. This loon pair successfully hatched two eggs but, according to a local observer, lost both chicks to a hawk on the long journey from the nest to water. Typically, loons will abandon their nest when dropping lake levels create such conditions, especially if the vertical distance up to the nest has changed dramatically. While loons can push themselves across mud flats, they have great difficulty climbing

Good example of "mud construction". The pair which used this nest was repeatedly harassed by eagles but did manage to fledge two chicks.
PHOTO BY WOODY HAGGE

The nest of the yellow-billed loon is usually much larger than common loon nests.
PHOTO BY EDGAR JONES

This nest in the Boundary Waters Wilderness Area is typical of small island nests—the distance to water is one push away.
PHOTO BY DAVE REPP

A pair of loons lined their nest with moss but abandoned this egg after seven weeks of incubation.
PHOTO BY WOODY HAGGE

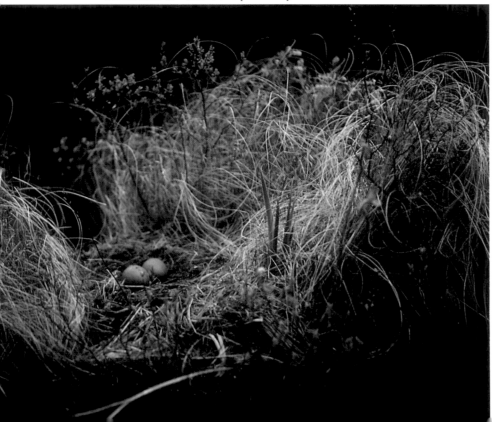

over obstacles such as exposed rocks or large logs. Problems associated with lake levels are particularly acute on reservoirs where hydroelectric dams raise and lower water levels to meet electric generation demands.

The Nest

Because nests are just small heaps of readily available vegetation, a common loon would never win a prize for either design or construction technique. After one nesting season, Sigurd Olson dissected a few loon nests and could not find a single material common to all the nests. Popular nest materials in his Minnesota wilderness study area were sweet gale, sedges and cedar boughs. Most likely, loons first select a site and then utilize whatever material is handy.

Loons are open-minded in their selection of the exact spot for their nest. Olson observed loons nesting on everything from sedge mats and floating muskeg to gravel bars and bare rock ledges. Often loons will plunk down right out in the open, making no attempt to camouflage their nest. Perhaps being large and aggressive compensates for such indiscreet behavior. However, many loons do build nests in heavy cover and attempt to keep their presence quiet and such loons probably have greater nesting success.

The loon nest is primitive, indicative perhaps of the loon's ancient heritage. There is no careful interlacing of materials or delicate placement of vegetation. Observing loons construct a nest, Judy McIntyre thought the placement of materials to be careless, a "lucky throw" when something landed in the right place. The loons she watched did not travel for any supplies; they simply pulled materials from within reach. Such an approach limits the physical dimensions of the nest. The largest nest McIntyre found weighed about forty pounds. Not much compared to an eagle's nest which crashed to the ground in Ohio years ago—it weighed over 4,000 pounds. Of course, that nest housed eagle families for about forty years, with each family, no doubt, doing

a little custom remodeling work. Common loons take a different view of home ownership. While they probably return to the same site each year, they do not salvage old nest materials. The nest from the previous year, if one can call a small pile of debris a nest, is usually destroyed by water and wind.

Often the nests of the yellow-billed and arctic loons, however, are used more than one season and are far more substantial. Living on tundra lakes with little relief, yellow-billed and arctic loons may need larger and consequently higher nests to provide a vantage point in the endlessly flat tundra country.

The nest building of the common loon does not consume a great deal of time. Judy McIntyre watched a pair of loons construct a nest over a four-day period. Recording the time the loons actually worked on the nest, McIntyre clocked the building project at three minutes shy of six hours. The male provided slightly more than half of the avian labor.

Eggs and Incubation

If the nest is neither high and dry nor flooded, loons have a good chance of hatching their eggs. Within a couple of days from the start of nesting, the female will lay her first egg. Observing a common loon lay her egg, McIntyre watched the loon's body rise up and down nineteen times before the egg appeared. Six minutes of what appeared to be voluntary expelling activity was required. After laying the egg, the loon panted and repeatedly opened and closed her eyes during a twenty-minute recovery period. Probably the degree of effort relates to the size of the egg. Loon eggs are quite large. Thirty loon eggs measured by Olson had an average length of 3⅜" inches and an average diameter of 2¼", about the size of the eggs of the white pelican, a larger bird. While their color varies tremendously, even within the same clutch, loon eggs are generally olive-brown

This remarkable series shows a loon turning the eggs and hatching a chick.

with dark brown or black splotches.

Typically, there is a one-day delay before a second egg is laid. Usually loons lay two eggs, but it's difficult to be definitive: a one-egg nest might well be the leftover from a nest which had an unwanted visitor, such as a gull, raven or raccoon. Looking at nests in northern Minnesota, Jim Titus counted seventy-three two-egg nests and fifty-six one-egg nests, roughly the sixty percent/forty percent split suggested by several other biologists. While a few three-egg nests have been documented, they are rare.

The egg or eggs must be incubated for about a month. While most bird books list the loon's incubation period at twenty-nine days, actual incubation time varies greatly. Scott Sutcliffe observed the incubation of several New Hampshire loons, finding an average incubation period of twenty-eight days with a range from twenty-five to thirty-three days. Recording the incubation periods of four Minnesota loons, Judy McIntyre found an average of twenty-seven days with a range of twenty-six to thirty-one days. (Knowing just when incubation begins is often a judgment call by the observer—it's rare for anyone to actually watch a loon lay an egg.)

While incubating, loons keep their eggs quite warm, around 95°F. While some birds like the penguin have a featherless brood patch, loons have a feathered area of their breast where blood vessels in the skin increase in size during incubation, better transferring the bird's body heat to the eggs. Like nest building, incubation is shared by the pair, a behavior common in birds. A loon pair shares nesting duties about equally. With stopwatch in hand, McIntyre estimated the average incubation bouts for common loons at just over two hours for the males and just under two hours for the females, who typically covered the late evening and early morning shifts. The length of each incubating session does not seem to follow a rigid pattern. Owen Gromme, a wildlife artist, recalls a pair of common loons which changed positions every half-hour; and others have recorded incubation duty shifts at random intervals.

One yellow-billed loon demonstrated an extreme devotion to nesting duty. Sverre Sjolander and Greta Agren watched a yellow-billed loon incubate a clutch for fourteen consecutive hours. They never heard this or any other yellow-billed loon call while on the nest, but common loons often prompt incubation duty changes with vocalizations. Olson remembers one loon which regularly revealed its fatigue or frustration by repeatedly broadcasting a long and mournful wail. After entering the nest, loons usually rearrange things slightly before settling in. On the nest they sit quietly, almost always face open water, and watch alertly with the head and neck extended.

Incubation doesn't appear to be stressful work. All loons need to do is turn their eggs occasionally. With awkward-looking but surprisingly efficient movements, loons turn the eggs at irregular intervals with partly open mandibles. Yellow-billed loons carry this irregularity to its extreme. Sverre Sjolander and Greta Agren recorded egg turnings at intervals ranging from twelve seconds to six hours. The typical turning interval for common loons is about an hour.

When loons are not turning eggs, they are just sitting; as yet, no one has reported a loon napping on the nest. Loons are faithful incubators. In 1919, naturalist Arthur Cleveland Bent commented that incubation " . . . is practically continuous; the eggs are never allowed to cool." In the 1970s, Judy McIntyre quantified "continuous" at ninety-nine percent. For each hour of incubation, loons in her studies were off the nest for only thirty seconds. Even in stressful circumstances, loons stick to the nest. In her doctoral dissertation on the common loon, McIntyre described a loon, "whose head could be seen crawling with blackflies," patiently sitting on the nest for over nine hours without relief. Trying to keep hordes of blackflies at bay, the loon shook its head an average of once every ten seconds.

The need for such stoic devotion to duty has been questioned by some biologists, citing evidence that loons have successfully hatched their eggs without a continuous

Adam Bayer of Fond du Lac, Wisconsin happened upon this loon chick while fishing in Canada. The following day he saw two chicks with an adult.

incubation effort. During the 1984 nesting season, the common loons on Massachusetts' Quabbin Reservoir were carefully monitored. Between July 1 and August 5, two nesting loons were watched on six occasions with the total observation time exceeding sixteen hours. A loon stayed on the nest for the full observation period on only one of the six visits. On July 29, a day of heavy boat traffic, a loon was on the nest just seventeen minutes during a three hour watch. Over the entire observation time, the loons were incubating only fifty-five percent of the time, yet the pair hatched two eggs and successfully raised two chicks.

Wisconsin photographer Woody Hagge also watched a pair of common loons break the incubation rules. On an unusually warm day in May a loon pair, though undisturbed, left the nest for several hours. Hagge presumes the departure was prompted by the discomfort of sitting on the nest in the blazing noonday sun. While loons are able to dissipate some excess heat by panting, sitting in direct sunlight could possibly overload a bird's cooling systems. Could it be these loons, with a wisdom acquired over millions of years, knew the eggs were okay? With the air temperature at 80°F, it is possible that the eggs were being incubated adequately by a substitute parent—the sun itself. Of course, the eggs were exposed to potential predation and the same loon wisdom should have encouraged the birds to at least stay near the nest. These loon eggs, by the way, did turn into loon chicks. Many eggs do not.

Predation

Predation takes a bite out of loon productivity. In most areas this is a natural part of the loon's life cycle. In some locales, however, predation has been the limiting factor in loon reproduction. On Lake Winnipesaukee up to eighty percent of the lake's egg production has been destroyed by raccoons. In 1975, this seventy square mile lake produced just one loon chick, and on nearby Squam Lake, raccoons

had about the same success rate. On both lakes, most of the destroyed nests were located within a few hundred yards of homes or other centers of human activity.

People and raccoons go together. Wherever there are people, garbage is not far behind, and behind the trail of garbage will be the friendly masked bandit, whose populations explode when their natural food supply is supplemented by human leftovers. In many resort areas the feeding of raccoons is encouraged because tourists love raccoons. Loons don't. Studying the effects of predation on loon productivity in Minnesota's Itasca State Park, Judy McIntyre found evidence of predation in over seventy percent of the unsuccessful loon nesting attempts. As in New Hampshire, the raccoon was loon enemy number one. Inspecting the nests destroyed by predators, McIntyre could implicate raccoons in seventy percent of the predation cases.

Raccoons, however, are not the only predators. The list of potential egg robbers is long, and includes crows, ravens, gulls, skunks, mink, otter, and possibly muskrat and beaver. Since some of these critters can destroy loon nests without leaving any tell-tale evidence, Judy McIntyre decided to experimentally identify potential predators. She built clever "track traps" by constructing a flat, smooth circle of sand and clay around former or simulated loon nests. In those nests she presented her bait—turkey eggs dyed to match the color of loon eggs. Raccoons loved this Easter egg party, showing up first eighty percent of the time. While this experiment does not prove that raccoons destroy eighty percent of all predated loon nests, it does provide strong circumstantial evidence that raccoons and loons, at least from a loon protector's perspective, don't mix.

Where raccoon numbers are low, as in remote wilderness areas, predation on eggs is not as serious a problem. A 1978 study by the Maine Audubon Society implicated predation in only three of eighteen nest failures. In northern Minnesota's wilderness lakes, Olson found evidence of predation in about half of all loon nests, but he carefully qualified his findings by suggesting that abandonment of the nest might have preceded the predation. If loons leave their eggs, predation at some point is almost inevitable. For a researcher covering a large study area, judging which came first is often speculative.

A quarter of a century after Olson's work, Jim Titus studied loons in the same area. For two years, Titus monitored every loon nest in the study area. Predation interfered with only twenty percent of the nesting attempts. Much lower than predation estimates from New Hampshire, this estimate reflects the relative scarcity of raccoons in the Minnesota wilderness, and explains Titus' data showing no difference in predation rates between island and mainland sites. In raccoon infested areas, islands are relatively safe nesting sites. While raccoons can swim, they rarely bother loons on small islands.

Avian Predation

Islands do not offer protection from avian predators. Titus believed crows and ravens were the major predators in Minnesota's wilderness areas. He found many loon eggs with puncture marks and even caught one crow red-handed in a loon nest. Believing ravens could actually fly off with a loon egg, Titus and a cooperative raven researcher working a nearby study area devised an experiment. They placed the largest chicken eggs they could find (turkey eggs were apparently hard to come by in northern Minnesota) in simulated loon nests. Then they watched ravens land, pick up a whole egg, and easily fly off. They presumed that ravens could also carry off slightly larger loon eggs. An investigation of raven nests in the area did turn up a positive identification of loon egg fragments. For Titus it explained why he rarely found successful loon nests near raven nests.

Where loons and gulls overlap nesting areas, loons often lose the battle for prime nesting sites. Titus frequently watched gulls harassing loons. In an attempt to protect its own territory, one gull set up house within three feet of an active loon nest; the loons quickly moved out. This could be a sign of the times. In recent years the increased levels of human activity in wilderness areas have provided more food for gulls. During twenty years of canoeing the Boundary Waters Wilderness Area of northern Minnesota and the adjacent Quetico Provincial Park, I have watched gull populations boom. It's not hard to figure out why. Quetico Provincial Park officials have been instructing fishermen to place fish remains on rocks near the shore. While this practice keeps campsites clean, it also creates fast-food stands for gulls. An expanding population is the price for their excellent scavenging services.

The common loon's predation problems are mild compared to those of the arctic loon. In a two-year study of the nesting success of arctic loons, Margaret Peterson estimated the nest failure rate at ninety-five percent one year and sixty-eight percent the next. Two avian predators, the long-tailed jaeger and the parasitic jaeger, were responsible.

Stickers or Flushers

Loons do not defend against humans. When people approach, loons will quietly slip off the nest and dive to a safe position. Typically, human intrusion does not provoke any displays unless the loon is caught by complete surprise. Some loons sit passively on the nest despite a close approach.

This tendency to sit tight varies greatly among bird species and individuals. The term *flushing distance* is used by biologists to describe a bird's tendency to flee. Trumpeter swans are quite touchy, flushing often at a hundred yards. Great blue herons are idiosyncratic, flushing at distances from fifteen to one hundred yards. Loons are more like great blue herons. Some loons abandon the nest at the first sign of a person while others refuse to budge even if some biologist is standing over them. Do loons realize their odds

Raccoons look cute but they can be a problem for loons. They love loon eggs.
PHOTO BY WISCONSIN DNR

The leftovers from a raccoon egg hunt. These eggs had been incubated for three weeks prior to predation. PHOTO BY WOODY HAGGE

of hatching eggs increase if they ignore those funny-looking two-legged animals with long black protruding eyes? That's doubtful.

Some loons just have more stick. Scott Sutcliffe met one loon who was either very tolerant or very stubborn. This bird would not move even as he approached within a couple feet. Maggie McGook, who graces several pages of this book, is such a loon. Named by Dr. Glenn Irwin, retired physician and loon photographer extraordinaire, Maggie is a classic sticker. Glenn can approach to within two or three feet without disturbing Maggie. While there is no tag on Maggie, Glenn is convinced that she (he knows Maggie is a she) returns to his lake every year.

Unpredictable But Persistent

It's always dangerous to generalize about loons, but after quantifying approaches to hundreds of loons, Jim Titus was able to catalog a few predictable behaviors, including a tendency of loons to flush more quickly if approached within their direct line of vision or if the movements of the person approaching are exaggerated or erratic. He also noticed that in the later stages of incubation loons sit tighter than loons just starting incubation. The most predictable response he uncovered was even more interesting: loons are not predictable at all, demonstrating a wide range of individual differences.

Loon eggs are not predictable either. Sometimes, despite adequate incubating, they simply do not hatch. Like many other birds, loons will try again. There are birds, termed indeterminate layers, which will keep laying eggs until some hatch. As an experiment, Arthur Cleveland Bent kept robbing eggs from the nest of a flicker. In forty-nine days, the poor bird laid thirty-seven eggs.

Loons are not that persistent. While they can lay up to four clutches, one re-nest is usually their best effort. And they will re-nest only if the egg or eggs are lost during the

Loon in the alert position.   PHOTO BY GLENN IRWIN

first half of the incubation period. Once an egg hatches, however, the re-nesting instinct dies.

Loons often move their nest site when they re-nest, especially if predators were involved in the first nest loss. Jim Titus found re-nesting attempts to be less successful than first nests. He believes first attempts are aided by greater nest attachment than later attempts. Titus rarely observed second re-nestings. Only three pairs out of a group of 112 pairs attempted a third nest. Even though the percentage of success is low, re-nesting is important for overall loon productivity. In Olson's study, thirty percent of all chicks hatched came from re-nests. Persistence pays.

Hatching the eggs is not the end of parental duties for loons. Loons take the tasks of caring for and feeding their offspring very seriously. With a month of incubation behind them, loons now look forward to about two months of family-raising responsibilities. A loon's work is never done . . . .

A Tale of Two Nests

Loons can hatch some memorable experiences. Ask Bruce Lutz, owner of the Newmann Lake Lodge in Price County, Wisconsin. A pair of Newmann Lake loons put Bruce in a difficult situation. For four years a pair of loons (he presumed the same pair) had nested on a small island. During the spring of 1984, high water levels forced the loons to build a nest about ten yards from their traditional spot. The nest was a good one and an egg was laid. But then the lake level dropped and the loons moved back to their "old" nest site, but naturally were unable to bring their egg along. A second egg was laid in the old, new nest. Two eggs, two nests, but one pair of loons.

The math didn't work too well and apparently the loons were not pleased with their decision. Lutz called Jim Pierce, Wisconsin Project Loon Watch coordinator, to report that the loons were spending a lot of time swimming between the two nests, calling almost continuously. The loons were upset. Lutz was upset.

Jim advised Lutz to wait until the loons settled upon one of the nests before attempting an egg rescue. The loons finally chose their old nest, abandoning the first egg. Then Bruce swung into action. He carefully picked up the abandoned egg, carrying it in a sheet of Saran Wrap, and brought it to the other nest. The loons were very suspicious. For about eight hours they would come near the nest, inspect it but quickly leave. Finally, early in the evening, one of the adults climbed onto the eggs and stayed put. Twenty-eight days later two chicks were hatched. Both survived their first summer. Lutz still enjoys watching loons but hopes his pair has learned to make up their minds about which nest is home. For his sake, as well as theirs.

PHOTO BY WOODY HAGGE

Raising a Family

"The majestic flight and mournful cry of this unique and complex bird once stirred the imagination and spirit of primitive tribes. More recently, the soul of modern man has also been captured by the sight and sound of this spectral bird winging through the evening dusk to its home and family."

—Joe Anderlik, 1978

The hatching of loon chicks is a cause for great joy—at least among humans. In New Hampshire, a tradition of celebrating hatchings with birth announcements has caught on, all apparently part of a "loon religion." That's a human response. What loons think, feel, or sense about the end of their incubation period will never be known. Anyway, that's a question for philosophers, not scientists.

The scientific community has, however, answered a lot of questions relating to the hatching and rearing of chicks. Scientists know that loon eggs, usually two, hatch about a day apart. Although it varies greatly by region, hatching dates typically occur during the last half of June. Scientists also know that loon chicks are precocial, being sufficiently developed at hatching to leave the nest quickly. Most ground-nesting birds like geese, ducks, grouse or cranes have precocial chicks, while tree-nesting birds like robins, bluebirds, owls or hawks have altricial or less developed chicks. For tree-nesters there is plenty of time to develop in the safety of a lofty nest. Not so on the ground, where chicks need to move out quickly before some predator stumbles onto the nest.

The First Days

For loon chicks the nest is home for only a very short time. After a half day of drying, chicks are capable of swimming. The first chick hatched will be called into the water with a soft call. After the second chick is hatched and dried, both chicks are lured to the water. Then the nest is abandoned. Usually neither the chicks nor the adults return to the nest, but there are exceptions. In 1984, a seasoned New Hampshire loon watcher observed an adult and a week-old chick climb up onto a nest to spend about ten minutes looking over the place the adult probably knew all too well.

Not all chicks make it out of the nest. During his 1984 field season in Maine, Paul Strong encountered three different nests where the dead chicks were still in their shells. Strong speculates that the pressure to remove the first

hatched chick might be strong enough to pull the adults off the nest early, thus abandoning the second chick. Any disturbance after the hatching of the first egg, including natural events such as a heavy rainstorm, could force the adults to abandon the nest and leave the second egg unhatched and fair game for crows, gulls or raccoons. Most loon researchers believe that the productivity of loons is reduced more by the failure of eggs to hatch than by the mortality of hatched chicks. Once hatched, most chicks survive. Scott Sutcliffe monitored the survival rate of New Hampshire loon chicks over a four-year period and found that eighty-four percent of all chicks hatched made it through the summer.

With sooty black down, except for the throat and upper breast which tends to be mouse-gray, a loon chick is a photographer's dream. The best description of young chicks dates back to 1906 when William Beebe, Curator of Ornithology at the New York Zoological Society, received an unusual gift of a one-day-old loon chick and a companion egg which was almost ready to hatch. Beebe was delighted with the opportunity to study birds which had never seen their parents or their natural environment. According to Beebe, the day-old chick pecked at everything and made low peeps much like a barnyard chick. When placed in water, the chick swam without hesitation and pushed its head completely underwater to look around at this new wet world. The chick did not appear to recognize live minnows swimming below, but did eat when fed small pieces of fish held by forceps.

A day after the first chick hatched, the other egg hatched revealing a loon chick sheathed, in Beebe's words, within a fine "hair-like wrapping of tissue" which required about three hours to split off. The chick helped by rolling on its back and scrambling around. At two days, the chicks were eating whole live minnows and each weighed about a quarter-pound. At three days they were preening and using the oil gland at the base of the tail. The only sound in the zoo environment which registered with the chicks was the call of the giant kingfisher. It threw them into fits of excitement, prompting Beebe to speculate that the similarity between the rolling call of the kingfisher and an adult loon's tremolo call stimulated the response. At one week of age the young loons finally captured two dying minnows. A day later the chicks pursued and caught live minnows. In the ninth day of this fascinating experiment, a sudden temperature drop on a chilly New York evening caused the death of both chicks.

Watching loon chicks in the wild is a pure delight. Their early attempts at diving are quite comical. I recall watching three-day-old chicks with their parents on Day Lake in northern Wisconsin. It was like watching diving ping-pong balls. The chicks tried to dive but their buoyancy made them pop right back to the surface. The deepest dive by two day old chicks is about a foot, but within a few days chicks can dive to depths of ten feet.

In 1982, Judy McIntyre published a paper in the *Journal of Field Ornithology* on the concept of nurseries. She had often observed the adults taking the chicks several hundred yards from the nest site to shallow, well protected areas. If there were adjacent loon territories, these "nurseries," as she termed them, were an average of 900 feet farther from other loon territories than the nest itself. McIntyre believes the young may "imprint", or identify behaviorally with a parent and thus with the proper species, during the zig-zag swim from the nest to the nursery. She never observed chicks being carried to the site. At least on her Saskatchewan study area, the nursery comprised about fifteen percent of the total territory. The bottom, under an average of about four feet of water, tended to be soft and mucky unlike the bottom at the nest site which is usually sand, gravel or rock. McIntyre feels nurseries play a critical role in chick rearing. Artificial nest islands, she suggests, should be placed near a potential nursery area.

While most chicks survive, they are vulnerable to the predation of northern pike, muskellunge or snapping turtles

The easy life! A chick just a few days old gets a free ride. This behavior prevents the chilling of chicks.   PHOTO BY WOODY HAGGE

from below and hawks or eagles from above. In Wisconsin, six years of volunteer population surveys have produced numerous reports of eagles attacking, but rarely taking, loon chicks. Woody Hagge, whose photographs in this volume speak for his close association with loons, has a dependable system for spotting eagles: loons tell him when an eagle passes over his lake by giving wild tremolo calls, even if it is well beyond the loons' nesting season.

The Care and Protection of Chicks

Because chicks are quite vulnerable to exposure and fatigue, chilling is a more serious problem than predation. According to McIntyre, body temperatures of chicks are about 7°F lower than the 102°F temperature of adults. This may be an important reason for the lengthy free rides adults give their chicks. Back-riding is a priceless sight seen only in the first few weeks of a chick's life. During the first week, the adults carry the chicks about sixty-five percent of the time. It saves the chick's energy and provides warmth. The free ride also offers the chicks protection from predators and allows the adults freedom of movement. To get on board, chicks often wait for the adult to partially submerge and lift its wings out of the way. To unload the chicks, the adult may dive quickly or rear back, leaving the chicks afloat and maybe a bit surprised. Some observers have watched chicks climb aboard without any help from the adults. Back-riding is not common with most other water birds, though grebes do carry their entire brood of three or four chicks at once.

The care and feeding of loon chicks is a full time vocation for the adults. In a doctoral dissertation on loons, Jack Barr estimated the energy requirements of chicks at eight times those of the adults. While studying yellow-billed loons, Sjolander and Agren watched the adults feed their chicks as frequently as seventy-three times during a single day. About fifteen percent of those feedings involved plant material. During the first twelve days of a chick's life, the two University of Stockholm researchers never saw them farther than six feet from the adults.

Although chicks start looking for fish early, they do not catch many until they are about a week old. Even at three weeks of age, chicks have a capture efficiency rate of only three percent, according to McIntyre. She has observed adults "teaching" fishing techniques to their chicks by dropping an injured fish or minnow in front of the chick. The feeding of chicks peaks at about two weeks and gradually drops off until the chicks at about eight weeks old can be considered independent.

In 1838, John James Audubon reported loons regurgitating food to feed their chicks. Unless loon behavior has changed since then, Audubon was mistaken. Chicks are fed small, live minnows between a half-ounce to one ounce in size after begging for food by pecking at the base of the adult's bill. Adults often dip the food in the water and splash it sideways before offering it to their young. With captive chicks, Olson discovered that food had to be presented in a similar fashion or the chicks refused to eat.

The early days for loon chicks appear to be easy ones, with time for feeding, riding on the adults' backs, loafing, preening and cruising—all with no apparent regularity. Olson once even observed a chick being fed by one adult while freeloading on the back of the other parent. What a life!

The level of parental care is impressive. When Olson captured chicks to mark them for his Minnesota study, the adults would perform spectacular displays, rushing up to within ten to twenty feet of the canoe while giving high-pitched tremolo calls. These protective efforts would last up to three minutes and would be repeated with decreasing intensity over a longer period. When the chicks were released, some parents immediately rejoined them while others offered "wary acceptance", but no chicks were rejected. Olson summed up loon parental behavior as "striking."

Loons are also known to accept orphan chicks. In June

This week-old chick is getting ready to abandon ship. At times chicks disembark without help from adults.
PHOTO BY WOODY HAGGE

of 1980, Wisconsin Department of Natural Resources wildlife biologist Ron Eckstein took a ten-day-old abandoned chick to a pair of loons with one chick. When the chick spotted the other loons, it immediately swam toward the new family. The adults escorted the chick to a nearby shoreline and within one minute the chick climbed on an adult's back, fully accepted. A month later, Eckstein observed the adult loons feeding two healthy chicks of about equal size. This foster-parenting role might explain reports of three-chick broods such as the one spotted in 1982 on Second Connecticut Lake in New Hampshire.

The protection of chicks continues for at least one month and in some cases up to three months. Adults with slow-moving chicks, one week to three weeks old, often employ a distraction display when threatened. If disturbed,

the adults will act as decoys, diving to open water and remaining conspicuous while the young lie flat on the water to lower their profile.

This behavior is similar to the broken-wing act of the blue-winged teal. While trout fishing on the Sioux River, a Lake Superior tributary, I encountered a teal flapping her wings and moving upstream just ahead of me. Entranced by her performance, I nearly missed seeing the brood of fuzzy chicks which were swimming quietly downstream tight against the bank, given away only by their "peeps." When I was about fifty yards upstream from our first point of encounter, I watched the teal recover miraculously and fly downstream to rejoin her brood. Female killdeer and ruffed grouse are famous for their performance of similar tricks.

Adult with three week-old chicks which have lost the dark down of younger chicks. PHOTO BY WOODY HAGGE

A six week-old loon trying (fairly successfully) to be invisible. Learning to "hide" on water extends the lives of many chicks. PHOTO BY WOODY HAGGE

Growing Up

At five or six weeks of age, loon chicks are nearly as large as the adults and simply dive away with them when threatened. As summer wears on, the chicks require progressively less attention. Not depending any longer on shoreline cover, by August the chicks will roam the entire territory. At ten weeks they are considered juveniles and their downy coats have been replaced with the drab-colored plumage of typical immature loons.

As with many other aspects of loon behavior, the adult/juvenile bond appears to be variable. As late as September, some juveniles remain with adults. While some juveniles may receive parental attention at this stage, the young loons can care for themselves. A turning point in the relationship between adults and juveniles is the development of flight feathers, which occurs at about eleven weeks of age. At this age, some immature loons leave their natal lake. Although McIntyre saw no young all summer on Lake Itasca in north central Minnesota, eleven juveniles were present by mid-September. She believes immature loons establish "autumn" territories on large lakes, retain distinct feeding areas, and often migrate together in pairs or small groups.

Some Notes on Productivity

Everyone wants "their" loons to hatch a pair of chicks, raise them successfully and go on to do it all over again every summer for the next twenty or thirty years. One biologist/mathematician determined that robins producing their typical two broods of four young each year would be responsible, counting the work of their offspring, for nineteen million robins over a ten year period. That's a lot of robins.

Using the same concept, but plugging in a different formula because loons only produce two young per year and the offspring don't breed for at least three years, a loon mathematician, assuming reproductive maximums, can project a total of 1,180 new loons over fifteen years. That total assumes several things: the first pair and all their offspring produce two chicks per year, every year; all young mature and reproduce at three years of age (their fourth summer); and none of the loons die.

Obviously it doesn't work that way with loons or any other wildlife species. Our lakes simply could not feed that many loons. While there are many factors which prevent populations from expanding in such geometric proportions, the most significant limitation in loon productivity is delayed breeding. Most birds and small mammals will breed within their first year and even large mammals like the whitetail deer will breed in their second fall. Although the breeding age of loons is not known with absolute certainty, most biologists believe loons are sexually mature in their fourth summer; six years must pass before the first grand-loons appear. Many biologists contend this delayed breeding period allows immature loons time to develop the fishing skills necessary to provide proper parental care later, but it certainly affects productivity. To continue their species, loons have to survive three winters in coastal waters where severe stress, disease and pollution cause significant mortality. Already the calculation of 1,180 loons is in jeopardy.

In addition, the significant number of loons which return north in breeding plumage but don't breed must be considered. There are quite a few territorial pairs that do not attempt nesting and a larger number of unpaired single birds, possibly very young or very old loons. Surveying

PHOTO BY WOODY HAGGE

This six week old loon developed a habit of demanding food with playful nips on the parents neck.   PHOTO BY WOODY HAGGE

Immature loons often stick very close to adults. Note how low loons ride in the water.   PHOTO BY WOODY HAGGE

Adult with very shy immature loon.   PHOTO BY WOODY HAGGE

Wisconsin's loons, Gary Zimmer classified twenty-eight percent of the entire population as non-breeding birds. Studies by Scott Sutcliffe in New Hampshire suggest that loons occupying the same territories each year will attempt nesting only three years in four, but will defend the territory in the off-year. Data from other studies support this theory. Studies in Minnesota and Alberta estimated that about twenty percent of the territorial loon pairs did not nest. Since the original calculation assumed that all three-year-old loons would reproduce, subtraction of at least twenty percent is in order.

Then there are egg loss and chick mortality; eggs and chicks face many dangers from predators. Another ten to twenty percent should be subtracted from the theoretical productivity.

Loons live in a real world, not a mathematical one.

The annual productivity of loons is measured as the number of surviving chicks per territorial pair. Obviously that number is not 2.0 with each pair contributing their fullest to the preservation of the species, but is typically within a range of 0.30 to 0.50, or thirty to fifty chicks per 100 pairs of adults. Considering historical data, one may expect 100 pairs of loons in the Boundary Waters Wilderness Area of Minnesota to produce forty-seven chicks; 100 loon pairs in New Hampshire to produce fifty-one loons and 100 pairs in Wisconsin to produce forty-eight chicks. For some areas the productivity is extremely low. In her 1978 study in north central Minnesota, Judy McIntyre found a productivity rate of 0.27, or twenty-seven chicks per 100 pairs.

When all the data on nesting success is reviewed, areas of special interest stand out. If loons are nesting in raccoon country, island locations are clearly more successful. In wil-

derness areas, however, location is not a factor. Titus found that smaller lakes produced relatively more young than larger lakes. He believed that the effort required to defend larger territories typical of large lakes might help explain the lower success rate. Smaller lakes in his Minnesota study area also had a considerably better ratio of loons to surface area of water: an average of one loon per forty-nine acres in small lakes, compared with one loon per 121 acres in large lakes.

According to Titus' data, the lucky loons are those in two-egg clutches. In his northern Minnesota study, eggs from one-egg nests had a mean of 0.21 chicks surviving per egg while eggs from two-egg clutches had a 0.40 mean rate of survival. So an egg has double the chance of producing a loon if it happens to have another egg next to it. While common sense might suggest loons could provide better incubation and care for a single egg and chick, common sense doesn't work well on this point. Olson's results were even more dramatic. Of nineteen one-egg nests only one succeeded, while fifteen of twenty-two of his two-egg nests produced chicks. He speculated that there might be less attachment, and therefore, less care for one egg than two.

While different studies show slightly different loon nesting success percentages, the nesting success average is about forty percent, which isn't bad when compared to other birds. In a 1979 study, Margaret M. Nice estimated a forty-nine percent success rate for all birds with open nests and a sixty-six percent success rate for cavity nesting birds. Common loons have a system that works. They have maintained viable populations for thousands of years. Given a little room, they will probably continue their survival game for thousands more.

Looking South

"The woodland lakes would be solitudes, indeed, did they lack the finishing touch to make the picture complete, the tinge of wilderness which adds color to the scene, the weird and mournful cry of the loon, as he calls to his mate or greets some new arrival. Who has ever paddled a canoe, or cast a fly, or pitched a tent in the north woods and has not stopped to listen to this wail of wilderness? And what would the wilderness be without it?"

—Arthur Cleveland Bent, 1919

The fall migration of loons is not a "here one day and gone the next" phenomenon. It's quite difficult to pin down a departure schedule because the migration process may begin as early as late July or early August when loons, at least to human eyes, begin to get restless. As summer wears on, the birds start a gradual movement from smaller to larger lakes, perhaps to find better fishing or to join other loons in pre-migratory flocks.

Birds of a Feather

On large northern lakes, it's tough to separate the early summer social flocking, often evident as early as mid-July, from the later pre-migratory flocking. In some areas, the two behaviors blend into each other. The early-season flocking usually occurs on large lakes where groups of a dozen or more loons assemble for afternoon sessions of cruising, preening and loafing. The early summer concentration sites often are used year after year. Of course, you have to be in high-density loon areas to find this behavior.

In July of 1976, Joe Anderlik found himself in very high-density loon country. He was fishing on 265-square-mile Molson Lake in northern Manitoba. He recalls that the weather had been lousy for several days but finally cleared, and days of ninety-degree heat followed. On the fourth day of the heat wave, the Cree guide motored the fishing party a considerable distance from their base camp. The lake was perfectly calm. Dozing off occasionally in the bow, Joe sat up quickly when he noticed a large congregation of birds. Instructing the guide to head toward the group of about 600 birds, Anderlik quickly realized he was watching his favorite bird, the common loon. Loons in the huge flock quietly preened as the boat passed. In over forty years of watching loons Anderlik had never seen anything like that assemblage. Few people have ever witnessed such a loon gathering, even once.

In the northwoods of Maine, Paul Strong sees flocks of loons nearly all season long. Groups of fifteen to twenty

Red-throated loon taking off.

are evident in his wilderness study area north of Baxter State Park as early as June. On small lakes the same flocking phenomenon occurs but with smaller numbers, usually four or five individuals. These groups are probably non-breeders or unsuccessful breeding pairs. They often stay together well into September when the early migrants decide to test their wings.

In his northern Minnesota wilderness study area, Sigurd Olson kept track of the total number of adult loons throughout the season and found a surprisingly steady decline. In June, he was seeing 109 to 114 adult loons. In late July, he counted 128 to 143 adults—the increase likely due to single loons and unsuccessful pairs moving in from other areas. In early September, however, he observed only eighty birds. By late September, he saw forty birds in the area and by early October he could find only twenty loons. Just a

few hardy loons stayed around until the late November ice closed the lakes. The juveniles followed a fairly similar pattern with twenty-one young on the scene in early September, fourteen in late September and ten in early October. Olson recalls the canoe country becoming strangely quiet as the hardwoods dropped their color. While coastal arrivals of loons have been observed in August on the Atlantic and late September off Florida's Gulf coast, most loons wait until late October or early November to head south.

For loon watchers, fall can be a time of mixed emotions. Are "your" loons just heading out for a feeding visit to another lake? Or are they leaving for the year and consequently leaving a big hole in your lake? It's hard to say good-bye to friends, even if you know they're going to warm, coastal waters. Unlike geese, which fly in large flocks, loons migrate singly or in small groups. Few people notice migrating loons. Given the typical early morning flights and the lack of calling, it is not surprising.

The First Leg

Many migrating loons may not be going far, at least at first. There are a number of traditional fall stopping places where large numbers of common loons gather for fairly short loon conventions. In Maine, October loon gatherings are quite predictable on some of the state's large lakes, like Pushaw near Bangor, and Great Pond near Belgrade, where groups of a hundred or more loons visit annually. A lake with only one or two nesting pairs, Trout Lake in northern Wisconsin hosts around fifty loons each fall, and New Hampshire's Squam Lake may accommodate fifty or more "guest" loons each fall, while nearby Lake Winnipesaukee provides for up to 100 extras. The Great Lakes provide several major gathering points like Kettle Point on Lake Huron, where every fall concentrations of hundreds or even thousands of loons can be viewed.

The best studied of the stopover lakes is Minnesota's Mille Lacs Lake, a shallow lake of 133,000 acres. In 1975, Judy McIntyre monitored loon movements during September, October and November. While over the summer Mille Lacs had just a few resident loons, during October there was considerable loon movement. By the third week of October, around 100 loons were present. During the final week of October, the population peaked at between 600 and 750 birds. By the end of the first week in November, nearly all the loons were gone. Residents of the area felt the build-up was normal, suggesting loons had always used the lake in this fashion.

Like the loons on the Maine and Wisconsin lakes, these were not local birds. If the numbers seem large, keep in mind the tremendous Canadian loon population. The large fall concentrations on the U.S. lakes could be loons coming from distant Canadian lakes to rest and refuel after their travels, adding a little fat by fishing on well supplied lakes. Mille Lacs, for example, is an extremely productive lake, and the Great Lakes stopping places could provide an abundance of alewives and smelt. From McIntyre's research on Mille Lacs Lake, it is evident that loons spend a lot of time feeding on these fall gathering lakes, termed "staging lakes" by scientists. From noon to about five o'clock, the loons spend most of their time feeding.

Once loons leave their staging areas they probably move quickly to the coast and then turn south, picking up their pace. During spring migration loons fly at a maximum speed of 93 mph, but reach flight speeds of 108 mph during the fall migration. Apparently winter's approach is a good motivator for loons. The final stimulus for the flight from the staging areas might well be weather. Most birds take maximum advantage of the wind, leaving when a wind from the northwest will give them a little help heading south. Some research doors concerning the migration of loons have yet to be unlocked, leaving the study of the roles of photoperiod, temperature and behavioral cues from other migrating birds as unexplored avenues for future study.

Not all loons make the big trip south. At least a few find the cold but open waters of the Great Lakes appealing enough to spend the winter. It's difficult, of course, to separate wintering loons from late migrants, but a U.S. Fish and Wildlife Service researcher did uncover some interesting evidence pointing to a Great Lakes wintering population. In October of 1983, Christopher Brand, a scientist at the National Wildlife Health Laboratory, was studying loon botulism mortality on Lake Michigan. Brand inspected forty of the nearly 600 loons estimated to have died during the outbreak. Of those forty loons only two had black and white breeding plumage. While the other thirty-eight birds fell into two distinct plumage types, examination of sex organs indicated that none of the thirty-eight loons were young-of-the-year. Most likely Brand was looking at immature loons which had spent their second or third fall on Lake Michigan.

In late summer and early fall, loons start to congregate, often in flocks of 100 or more.
PHOTO BY R.C. BURKE

Problems En Route

Some loons try heading south but have a hard time. Loons seem to have a fatal fascination for wet highways, and reports of loons attempting to land on rain-slick roads are common. In 1982, sixteen immature loons tried to land on highways near Rhinelander, Wisconsin. It was a windy and snowy November evening. Between 7:00 and 8:00 p.m., the loons started dropping on blacktop roads. Apparently the glare from car headlights gave the roads the appearance of rivers; no loons were found along the many miles of gravel roads in the area. Of the sixteen birds, thirteen were successfully treated by the Northwoods Wildlife Center in nearby Minocqua and returned to open water.

While not all loons are given such a second chance, another loon traveling through Wisconsin had luck on its side. On New Year's Eve of 1982, an immature loon crash landed next to a farmer's barn near Antigo in northeast Wisconsin. The Northwoods Wildlife Center again did some minor repairs and sent the loon south early in the new year.

Some loons flying down the East coast have had similar problems. In early December of 1984, nine loons decided to land in some unusual places in suburban Maryland. One landed in the parking lot of a shopping center, another in a swimming pool in Bethesda and one dropped down on the runway of an airport. All nine loons, eight common and one red-throated, were rescued and treated at The Chesapeake Bird and Wildlife Sanctuary in Bowie, Maryland. Some had bleeding feet but all were released to the waters of Chesapeake Bay.

A few loons wait a little too long before starting their flight south. In November of 1979, on Tiger Cat Flowage near Hayward, Wisconsin, another immature loon became trapped when ice started closing in on it. Since loons cannot run on ice to take off, this bird was doomed. Two Wisconsin Project Loon Watch staff members arrived at the lake with a canoe, paddles, an axe, a flashlight and a landing net. Three hours later they captured the reluctant loon, needing every piece of equipment and some luck to get the loon out of the rapidly freezing water of the lake. After spending a comfortable evening in a bathtub at Northland College in Ashland, the loon was tagged and released to the open waters of Lake Superior.

Not all the loon-trapped-in-the-ice stories have such happy endings. An immature yellow-billed loon near Prudhoe Bay in northern Alaska did not pick up on nature's cues. The freezing lake closed in on the loon, but the ice was not solid enough to allow an attempted rescue by a nervous lakeside family. For about a week a pair of adult yellow-billed loons flew over the stranded bird daily, but did not land in the small patch of water. The adult birds, presumably the parents, attempted through vocalizations to get the young loon off the lake, but it was too late. Finally

PHOTO BY TOM KLEIN

the adults left and natural selection played out its ancient role.

Empty Lakes

After the last loon has left a northern lake the silence is complete, almost painful. There is still life on most lakes, a few bluebills passing through perhaps or a lingering kingfisher, but it's not the same. Bent had it right in 1919: the woodland lakes would be "empty solitudes" without the cry of the loon. The North's loss is the South's gain. While loons are not as attractive in their gray winter plumage, they do add to the diversity of bird life on coastal waters. The exact overland routes from the upper midwest are not known for certain. For most northeastern loons the trip south follows the Atlantic coast. Loons in Alaska and the Canadian northwest take a general southwest flight path to the Pacific coast wintering areas.

Some day a radio telemetry study of loon migration will provide exact information on the routes loons take. Such a study might even provide clues regarding the relationships between weather and fall migration, or food supply and fall migration. But telemetry will never offer a single clue to help mortals understand why it hurts a little to see loons head south for a long winter.

Winter Vacation

"The loon's natural environment is northern. When they're out of their natural environment, they're just another bird."

—Joe Anderlik, 1984

Loons and winter? It's not quite like love and marriage, or Friday and fish fries. Interest in wintering loons is somewhat like Christmas sales of air conditioners in Bangor—a little restrained. It's no surprise. The striking summer bird of the north with the beautiful voice becomes a drab, shy coastal resident. The two things northerners love about loons—the dramatic plumage and the haunting calls—are not enjoyed by southerners. After the late fall molt, the northern postcard loons just aren't the same.

I recall sitting on a Key West boardwalk watching an immature loon feed and loaf in the warm, shallow waters. Several tourists stopped to politely ask what I found so interesting. I offered the spotting scope. Two of them responded with a statement something like, "What a funny looking duck, is it rare?" These "ducks" are typically very quiet on the wintering grounds. While a two-week exploration of the Keys in 1983 produced many loon sightings, not a single loon was heard calling. Many northern loon lovers who spend each winter in Florida wait patiently for the calling they love so deeply up north. Few are rewarded. Loons do vocalize in some areas of their wintering range, but it's not as predictable or as sustained as in their summer environment.

Loon religion has not invaded the Deep South. Even bird groups there don't give the loon much more than a passing interest. In 1982, Jim Pierce of Wisconsin Project Loon Watch and Jeff Fair of the New Hampshire Loon Preservation Committee tried to organize bird groups in southern coastal areas to provide loon population data. The response was as lukewarm as Florida tidal pools. Another effort to organize professional and amateur ornithologists in 1984 met with similar disinterest. Of 850 birders asked to provide information on wintering loons, only fifty-five responded. And just try to find loon postcards, tee-shirts, ties or whiskey glasses in Florida, Texas or the Carolinas!

While the highest concentrations of wintering common loons on the East coast are found off the North Carolina, Virginia and Maryland coasts, loons can be found in almost all coastal waters from Maine to Texas. T. A. Imhof, a University of Alabama researcher, estimated the 1977 wintering population at over 10,000 in an area from the mouth of the Mississippi to St. Mark's, Florida.

On the West coast, where the loon populations from Alaska and western Canada winter, the estimates are much higher. Approximately 12,000 loons of three species (common, red-throated and arctic loons) spend the winter off the Washington coast, according to Kelly McAllister of Washington's Non-Game Office. Bill Haight, an Oregon Non-Game official, termed loons "abundant" in the coastal estuaries of that state. Loons of all four species winter along California's 800-mile coast and John Gustafson of the California Non-Game Department receives reports of common loons wintering on inland lakes and reservoirs of the state.

A survey completed in the spring of 1984 added considerably to our knowledge of winter loon movements. Coordinated by Judy McIntyre, the survey indicated a northward movement of loons along the Atlantic coast during the winter. In January and February, the greatest concentrations of loons were found off the coast of South Carolina. In March, the largest groups were observed off the New Jersey coast. In April, the concentrations moved up to the Massachusetts and New Hampshire shores. Both north-south and inshore-offshore movements were noted along the west coast of Florida, normally an area of substantial loon numbers. On the Texas coast, loons were seen in modest numbers in January and February but by March a pre-migration buildup had occurred.

It is impossible to know at this time if loons from a given nesting region travel to a specific wintering site. There would be an adaptive survival value for loons from geographically distinct populations to spread out all over the coast. The potential for a single catastrophe involving disease, pollution or a violent storm to affect an entire population would be reduced. We do know that winter is a time of great stress for the loons and it is on the coastal waters

that natural selection does its work. McIntyre terms winter mortality "considerable." Of nine loons she banded between 1970 and 1973, three died during their first coastal winter.

Malcolm Simons, Coordinator of the Atlantic Beached Bird Survey which monitors bird mortality along the U.S. coasts from northern Massachusetts to Texas, has termed loon mortality in winter "out of proportion to its population throughout its coastal ranges." Started in 1975, the Beached Bird Survey utilized volunteers to walk stretches of coast tallying the dead seabirds they encountered. During the first four years of the survey, loon mortality was low but, according to Simons, it increased steadily until the major loon die-off in 1983 when loons accounted for over seventy percent of all the birds found. While Simons cites severe weather as the greatest cause of seabird mortality, he does not ignore pollution, especially oil spills. Looking at all the survey records, he estimates that about seven percent of all loons found were oiled. The 1983 sinking of the *Marine Electric* off the Florida coast resulted in thirty-two loon deaths and an additional 134 oiled loons required assistance.

Pollution in winter habitats is not easy on loons, and adjusting to salt water may be an added stress. Like many other birds utilizing the marine environment, loons are able to cope with salt water by secreting excess salt through a nasal gland. Not found in songbirds, the "salt gland" is used by cormorants, grebes, herons, gulls, terns and loons to limit the salt concentration in the blood to about one percent, approximately one-third of the salt concentration of sea water. This marine bird adaptation was first identified in 1957. Although some avian physiology textbooks do not list the loon among the thirteen orders of birds possessing a functional salt gland, researchers at the Fish and Wildlife Service's National Wildlife Health Laboratory in Madison, Wisconsin have located the gland in common loons.

The most detailed single study of wintering loons was conducted by Judy McIntyre in 1978 near Assateague Island, Virginia. With highly productive waters supplying an abundance of fish and shellfish, the Assateague Island study area provided a nearly ideal habitat for wintering loons. McIntyre found that as in summer, loons in winter will mix with other loons but rarely with other species. By carefully watching for individuals with distinctive markings, such as one loon with a bent bill, McIntyre determined that loons utilize distinct feeding territories. Each loon, not each pair as in summer, has its own area and defends it with displays and occasional vocalizations.

Wintering loons spend just over half of their daylight hours feeding. Preening and other maintenance activities take up another quarter of their day, with the balance spent drifting and sleeping. Apparently the tides are important for feeding loons, bringing in new, unsuspecting prey twice a day. All of the loons McIntyre observed fed in the early morning and mid-afternoon with a final surge in late afternoon. The feeding activity usually includes at least some bottom feeding since shellfish were brought to the surface on several occasions. There are reports in British bird journals of wintering loons feeding heavily on crabs. North American loons, especially when stormy weather creates turbid water conditions, will also feed on crabs. During McIntyre's study, she never observed flock feeding: spaced about 150 yards apart, the birds always fished as individuals. In winter, feeding dives averaged just under forty seconds, only three seconds shorter than average summer dives timed by McIntyre. With ample prey available, the loons typically stayed in a protected area all day and kept fairly regular habits.

Those habits included flocking at sunset when a raft of about 100 loons would form about twenty minutes after sunset. While the exact location varied, the raft could be seen in the same general area—the deepest part of the cove—each evening throughout the winter. Given the extensive evidence that loons are sight feeders, it is doubtful that loons feed at night either in winter or summer. A spurt of feeding

at low tide is probably stimulated by the concentration of potential prey as the water recedes. This abundance of prey probably accounts for the relatively small winter feeding territories of ten to twenty acres in winter, as contrasted with the summer territories of five to ten times that size.

The function of evening rafting is anyone's guess. It is unlikely that safety in numbers is the answer. On coastal waters loons have few enemies, except possibly the thresher shark. McIntyre suggests the rafting could simply be a behavior which keeps the birds offshore and prevents possible strandings on the beaches in storms. Another possibility she suggests is more subtle. If the loons stay together the probability of roughly synchronous spring departure and subsequent arrival on the breeding grounds increases. This would force all birds to play by the same rules and give none an advantage of early nesting site selection. But since the actual arrival on northern lakes is usually preceded (at least for midwestern and Canadian loons) by a series of stagings on any available open water, the necessity to leave together is questionable.

Even when defending their winter feeding territories, loons seldom call. During her research at Assateague, McIntyre heard the yodel occasionally and the tremolo only twice. The melancholy wail apparently is reserved for the solitude of the summer lakes.

The population of wintering birds reaches all the way to Maine. Along the Maine coast a winter survey is conducted annually by the Maine Audubon Society. In 1983, about 300 loons were sighted. Since some areas of the coast were not covered, the total coastal population is probably in the range of 500 birds. The majority of Maine's approximately 3,000 summering loons decide, like many other Maine residents, to spend the winter in a slightly warmer clime. According to Maine Audubon's Jane Arbuckle, Maine's wintering loons do spend the entire season off the Maine coast braving the famous, bitter nor'easters. Paul Strong, one of the cooperators in the winter census, reports that the Maine winter population is composed primarily of single birds and small groups of from two to six loons. He also reports that, at least in Maine, the wintering loons are silent. Over several years of monthly coastal observations, he has yet to hear a loon calling. It may well be that the calling reported by McIntyre occurs only where large concentrations of loons are present. Or it could be that Maine loons are like the stereotypical Maine residents—strong and silent.

Clearly, loon numbers on the wintering grounds are not what they were in 1907 when Frank Chapman, author of *Handbook of Birds in Eastern North America*, noted in his journal: "They winter in large numbers some distance off the coast. I have seen several thousand in a day east of Hatteras when sailing from New York to Florida."

Mystery loon. This common loon in immature plumage was photographed in June of 1982 on Lake Tomahawk in northern Wisconsin. Either it was an adult which acquired its breeding plumage very late, or it was a one or two year old loon which came north "early".   PHOTO BY WOODY HAGGE

A loon in winter plumage enjoying the sunshine in the placid water off Key West.
PHOTO BY TOM KLEIN

Looking Ahead

Hanging On

"The plight of the loon takes many forms, often human-induced: artificial water level fluctuations that flood or strand vulnerable nests; predation; loss of nesting habitat to development; disturbance during the nesting season. The most insidious threat of all is acid rain, which has already killed hundreds of lakes, and will destroy all life in many more unless its sources are controlled."

—Jeff Fair, 1983

It's a tough world for loons. They have battled diseases, competition from other species, high and low water levels, predation and other natural threats for millions of years—and survived them all. During the past few decades, however, *Homo sapiens* hasn't made the loon's lot any easier. While the sport shooting of loons is thankfully a sad memory, a frightening list of new and more insidious problems are facing the bird: toxic chemicals, acid rain, destruction of nesting habitat, nest flooding, increased predation caused by the exploding populations of some predators, commercial fishing operations which net loons in addition to fish, and harassment by people. None of these problems faced loons when Native Americans developed their versions of loon religion. Some are serious enough to threaten the very existence of the species; others are just nagging problems in restricted geographic locales. But all must be dealt with if the cry of the loon is to be heard in the twenty-first century and beyond.

Chemical Contamination

The story of chemicals and birds has always been disturbing. While most of the more than 60,000 man-made chemicals in our environment do not cause problems, at least a few are potentially dangerous. The role of dichloro-diphenyl-trichlorethane (DDT) in the population declines of the eagle, osprey and peregrine falcon is well documented. At high levels, DDT prevents the eggshells of these and other birds from reaching normal thickness, and when a nesting bird sits on its thin-shelled eggs, the eggs are crushed. Synthesized in 1874 but used widely only during and after World War II, DDT was called a modern miracle.

For a time it controlled mosquitoes and other pests, but the miracle was short-lived. Pests developed resistance, even immunity, to the toxin. By the 1960s, a few people saw the tip of the DDT iceberg. In 1962, Rachel Carson's *Silent Spring* alerted the public to the dangers of indiscrim-

Levels of mercury in loon eggshells are increasing, but to date productivity has not been affected.   PHOTO BY GLENN IRWIN

breeding in the United States, 332 species spend the winter in tropical areas of Mexico, the West Indies, Central and South America—all areas where DDT is still used.In the northern half of the Midwest, decreases in the eggshell thickness of many birds, including eagles, have been documented. Studies by University of Wisconsin researchers Joseph Hickey and Raymond Faber indicated eggshell thickness decreases in nine of thirteen fish-eating species when shells from 1970 were compared with museum samples collected before 1946. In great blue herons, the eggshell thickness decrease was twenty-five percent. Black terns, double-crested cormorants, herring gulls and red-breasted mergansers had shell thickness decreases of thirteen to twenty-three percent.

Fortunately, loons have not as yet been as seriously affected. In a *Wilson Bulletin* article, Scott Sutcliffe reported an eleven percent decrease in loon eggshell thickness when comparing 1978 eggs from Squam Lake and Lake Winnipesaukee in New Hampshire with museum samples. The level of DDT present correlated with the thickness of the shell—the higher the level of DDT, the thinner the shell—but the differences were slight. The average thickness of the fourteen 1978 eggs was 0.59 mm while the museum samples, all dating to a pre-DDT era, had an average thickness of 0.65 mm. According to Sutcliffe, the eggshell thinning problem had little or no effect on loon productivity in New Hampshire.

Canadian research has also demonstrated the presence of chemicals in loons. Eggs collected in 1970 were significantly thinner than thirty-nine eggs from The Royal Ontario Museum which were collected before 1947. More importantly perhaps, the more recent loon eggs contained traces of DDT, Mirex, PCB, dieldrin and mercury. Mercury levels in eggs from the Algonquin Park area were quite high, 1.11 parts per million (ppm) in one case.

Contaminants were found in loons too. As reported in the *Journal of Environmental Contamination and Toxicology,*

inate DDT use and indirectly launched the environmental movement. By the mid 60s, the spectacular peregrine falcon had disappeared from much of its range, a victim of DDT. The osprey, once a familiar East coast raptor, declined rapidly, as did the bald eagle. In 1972, the Environmental Protection Agency banned DDT in the United States, but DDT is still being used in other parts of the world. While the worldwide situation is improving, many birds now pick up DDT in their wintering habitats. Of the 650 species of birds one group of investigators analyzed 204 loon carcasses found between 1969 and 1979. Except for a few that were shot or died from swallowed fishhooks, these loons drowned in commercial fishing nets. Of the 204 loons, thirty were found in an emaciated condition. Of these thirty, seven loons had lethal levels of mercury and one a very high level of lead. All of the loons had evidence of at least some DDT, PCB, dieldrin and mercury contamination, but the levels in the emaciated loons were significantly higher than in the 174 non-emaciated loons. The levels of mercury in the livers of healthy, juvenile loons, for example, averaged 1.92 ppm while the average in emaciated juveniles was 26.4 ppm. For adults, the equivalent numbers were 6.35 ppm in healthy loons and 16.3 ppm in emaciated birds.

Loon feeding habits may offer some protection from DDT and other toxic chemicals. Because toxic chemicals can work their way up through the food chain by a process of bio-accumulation, chemicals in lake water may be present at a relatively harmless level of parts per trillion, but when microscopic zooplankton absorb the chemicals, the contaminants can be concentrated to parts per billion. And when small minnows and fish eat the zooplankton, the concentrations can reach parts per million. When predator fish eat small prey, they store this cumulative contamination in their fat tissues; so, an eagle feeding on the carcass of a large fish can get a heavy dose of chemicals. Since loons usually feed in a safer area of the food chain, they do not pick up nearly the contamination absorbed by eagles or ospreys feeding on large prey.

Wildlife managers are showing concern but not panic over the growing body of scientific evidence documenting the presence of chemical contaminants in loons. While the jury is still out, scientists do know that loons are carrying fairly high levels of PCB and mercury. The fact that loons continue to reproduce despite their body burden of chemicals and metals is no cause for joy; it might just buy them a little more time.

While disease kills thousands of loons on coastal waters, mortality on inland lakes is rare.   PHOTO BY TOM KLEIN

Botulism

A little more time is something disease rarely gives its victims. Probably more loons have died from disease than all other causes. In the 1960s alone, Type E botulism killed at least 10,000 common loons. A silent and efficient killer, botulism has been a major cause of waterfowl deaths, killing in 1952 five million ducks in the western United States. Botulism is a disease caused by the ingestion of food contaminated by toxin from the bacterium *Clostridium botulinum.*

In its spore stage, this microorganism is not a problem, but under the proper conditions—suitable nutrients, favorable temperature and the absence of oxygen—a very powerful toxin is produced. If loons pick up this pre-formed toxin by eating contaminated baitfish, they can be killed by the toxin. There are six types (A through F) of botulism: Type E is no friend of loons.

Major epidemics (termed *epizootics* by wildlife scientists) of Type E have visited Lake Michigan repeatedly, destroying thousands of loons; eight major autumn outbreaks have occurred between 1959 and 1983 and the outbreaks of 1963 and 1964 alone killed an estimated 6,870 loons. The diagnosis of botulism E was definite. When laboratory mice were injected with blood serum from dead loons, the mice died. When the mice were first given Type E anti-toxin, they lived. While gulls and other water birds were affected in these fall die-offs, common loons were most severely affected. Why loons? Fall is the time for the annual pre-migratory flocking and Lake Michigan has several traditional staging areas where hundreds or even thousands of loons congregate.

Just how the disease is transmitted is perplexing. Normally loons eat only live fish, and botulism toxin is rarely present in samples of live, healthy fish. Possibly, loons eat sick baitfish in which the levels of the botulism toxin are present but low. Since botulism is not a significant problem in most of the loon's range (Lake Michigan has had the only major occurrences), the resistance of loons to botulism is probably very low. Some bird species, like the turkey vulture whose appetite for carrion is well-known, can resist 100,000 times as much Type C botulism as a pigeon. Although loons haven't been tested, they would, no doubt, be closer to pigeons in their resistance to botulism.

A study of a 1983 botulism outbreak, conducted by the U.S. Fish and Wildlife's National Wildlife Health Laboratory in Madison, Wisconsin, concluded that between October 10 and 31 at least 582 loons died of botulism Type E in the Lake Michigan waters off the Garden Peninsula. Because of probable removal by scavengers and winds which kept many dead birds offshore, the mortality estimate is conservative. As many as twenty-two dead birds per mile washed up on the beach.

Laboratory tests confirmed the presence of botulism E, but could not pinpoint the source. The possibility of contamination from large numbers of dead pink salmon was considered, but since loons are not scavengers this theory was rejected. Five species of baitfish found on the beach were collected and analyzed; three species—burbot, alewife and smelt—tested positive for botulism E. Both smelt and alewife are common loon prey. While there is a possibility that the botulism toxins formed after the baitfish died, there is a stronger possibility that moribund prey, with botulism E, were eaten by loons.

National Wildlife Health Lab researcher Christopher Brand commented in an interview that no feasible control or prevention methods yet exist to protect loons from botulism. The bacteria will always be present and loons, most likely migrants from Canadian nesting areas, will likely return to their traditional stopping places en route to the Atlantic or Gulf coasts. Since it would be impossible to keep loons off thousands of square miles of Lake Michigan, botulism E may continue to be an unavoidable and substantial source of natural loon mortality.

The Florida Die-Off

According to a March, 1984 *Audubon* magazine article by Frank Graham Jr., the first victim of the "Florida die-off" washed ashore on January 4, 1983 at Dog Island, a 1800-acre barrier island on the northern Gulf coast of Florida. Many more followed. By early February, ten to twenty dead or dying loons came to Dog Island's beaches. All along the Gulf coast the story was repeated, hundreds of times a day. While the U.S. Fish and Wildlife estimate of the total

One of the victims of the "Florida Die-off".   PHOTO BY ROBERT LANGE

mortality was 2,500, some observers in Florida believed the total mortality was much higher, perhaps as high as 10,000. Smaller numbers of loons died along the Virginia and North Carolina coasts.

Most of the dead loons were in an extremely emaciated condition—some had a body weight of under three pounds, about a third of a loon's normal weight. A Dog Island regular and field researcher for The Nature Conservancy, Bob Alexander saw many loons in that condition. Watching a Fish and Wildlife scientist perform a field necropsy, Alex-

ander was startled to see birds which, in his words, "lacked the very stuff of life. You cut them open, and you didn't find the basic things a bird needs to survive: muscles, blood and food."

Even after two years of study, the die-off perplexes scientists. They know more about what it wasn't than what it was: it was not caused by botulism, an oil spill, nor any clearly defined pollutant. As in any good mystery, though, there are a few clues.

One of the clues found by Bob Lange, a U.S. Fish and Wildlife scientist working on the case, was the presence of mercury and selenium in the tissues of dead loons. Of sixteen loon livers analyzed, nine had mercury concentrations of greater than 20 ppm, considered a "danger zone" by scientists. Mercury has long been known to be bad medicine for wildlife.

These loons apparently did not die of mercury poisoning per se. In an unpublished report on the die-off, Fish and Wildlife Service scientists concluded: "We do not believe a diagnosis of mercury poisoning can be substantiated as a general diagnosis for loon deaths over such a wide area." They termed mercury "contributory" to the emaciated condition of the birds.

Also termed contributory were the large numbers of *microphallidae* (internal parasites) found in the loons. These parasites, according to Lange, were found in incredibly high numbers. Normally present in loons at levels measured in hundreds, the parasites were found in the dead Florida loons at levels of up to 80,000. Such parasite burdens could have easily killed the loons. But the story doesn't end there. Healthy loons have no business feeding on the grass shrimp or mole crabs (not blue crabs as previously reported) which probably are the hosts to this parasite.

If the loons were in a weakened condition, however, they might have stopped feeding on fish, swam to shallow water and started feeding on the grass shrimp or mole crabs. Enter mercury. While this is only a theory, it is possible, even likely, that the loons suffered from central nervous system damage due to the mercury in their systems. Bob Lange recalls that many of the loons he observed during the die-off acted blind and demonstrated behaviors which to him were not consistent with simple weakness due to the parasite problems.

Mercury is widespread in the environment, and over the past thirty years, mercury in eggshells has greatly increased; it is now found in the shells of most fish-eating birds, including the shells of loons. In twenty-one New Hampshire loon eggs, the mercury content averaged 0.54 ppm, a level above the 0.5 ppm "concern level" for ring-necked pheasants and near the 1.0 ppm concern level for most waterfowl. Some loon eggs from the New Hampshire sample did have over 1.0 ppm of mercury. Unlike many other contaminants such as DDT or PCBs, mercury levels in loon eggs have not decreased in recent years.

But unlike mysteries which tie-up nicely with a confession in the last chapter, this story is complicated by Dr. Donald Forrester from the University of Florida's College of Veterinary Medicine. He had the vision to look at healthy loons a year after the die-off. In 1984, a few loons were collected and analyzed for mercury. These loons had levels of mercury similar to the loons which died the year before. But no loons died on the Florida beaches in 1984. Like everyone else who has looked at the issue, Forrester is confused by the findings. In 1983, some other factors—inadequate prey populations or weather conditions possibly—must have worked with the mercury to start the chain of events ending in the destruction of thousands of loons.

So there is not enough information yet to write the final chapter in the Florida die-off/mercury story. While the connections between mercury levels and acid rain have yet to be clearly demonstrated, circumstantial evidence suggests an interplay. It is known that under the effect of strongly acidic rain, mercury commonly present in soil and rock can be released. When the acidity of rainfall is strong enough

to break the chemical bonds holding the metal, mercury can be percolated into a lake or river making it available for fish and wildlife to absorb. This has happened in Scandinavian countries where several heavy metals including mercury have been implicated in serious fish and wildlife problems. If acid rain is increasing the levels of mercury in the northern breeding range, the Florida die-off becomes a bit less mysterious but far more ominous. Alone, mercury probably does not kill loons, but combined with the stress of migration, storms and parasites, it could be a silent killer.

Loons on parade: adult with ten week old immature loon.
PHOTO BY WOODY HAGGE

Acid Rain

Of all the threats facing the loon, acid rain is the most serious. Jeff Fair of the New Hampshire Loon Preservation Committee calls it the "most insidious" threat to loons. Rawson Wood, Chairman of the North American Loon Fund, terms it the "most urgent issue for loons." Nearly all scientists, even electric company scientists, admit that there is an acid rain problem, but there is considerable debate regarding the specific solutions, timing and costs of control measures. While most coal and utility representatives argue for more research and no action, environmental groups point

out that every nation in the western world, except the United States, is committed to at least a thirty percent reduction of acid-causing pollutants (SO_2 and NO_x gases). Indeed, several United States scientific organizations, including the National Academy of Sciences, recommend an immediate control program.

This debate is critical for loons. It requires little scientific sophistication to realize that fishless lakes will become loon-less lakes. Because they mainly feed on rough fish and minnows which are less sensitive to acid rain than most game fish, loons might stay around after a lake's walleye and trout populations have disappeared, but don't look

The area of acid-sensitive lakes overlaps the common loon's breeding range (see page 33 for comparison). PHOTO BY E.P.A.

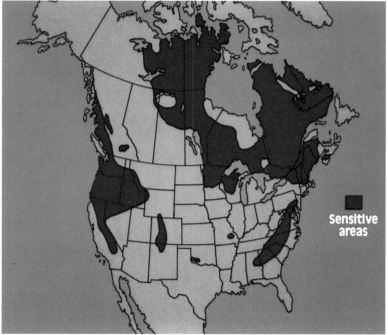

Liming of lakes can protect waters threatened by acidification, but it is expensive and long-term biological affects are not well understood. PHOTO BY U.S. FOREST SERVICE

for loons on the nearly 200 acidified Adirondack lakes. Unfortunately, the maps of acid-sensitive lakes and the maps of the common loon's breeding range overlap all too well. Both cover the Laurentian Shield like a blanket of acidic snow. Acid rain must be dealt with, not just for loons, but for all wildlife.

Commercial Fishing

Nets set for trout or other game fish often catch more than fish. Deep-diving loons entangle themselves in nets with all too frequent regularity. In 1960 and 1961, a combined total of about 5,000 common loons died in nets on Great Slave Lake in the Northwest Territories. While losses on the Great Lakes do not reach that level, John Lerg of the Michigan Department of Natural Resources reported at a 1981 loon conference in Minneapolis that a "substantial" number of loons are killed in Michigan waters of Lakes Superior and Michigan through commercial fishing operations. Others in the Michigan DNR have termed the mortality "very high," but do not provide numerical estimates. Commercial fishermen working the waters off the Garden Peninsula in Lake Michigan are responsible for most of the Great Lakes common loon mortality.

Hydro Power Water Levels

Loons require relatively stable water levels for successful nesting. Fluctuating water levels caused by hydroelectric dams can be detrimental to loon populations. The problem is particularly acute in the Northeast where hydro developments control the levels of many important loon lakes. New Hampshire's Lake Umbagog is a case in point. According to a long-time lake resident Armand Riendeau, Lake Umbagog's wildlife, especially ducks and loons, has suffered in some years from the policies of the company owning the water rights on the river systems feeding the sprawling wilderness lake. Riendeau claims up to ninety percent of the nesting ducks have been lost in some years to nest flooding. Despite the presence of eleven common loon nests on Umbagog in 1978, chick production was zero. This prompted the New Hampshire Loon Preservation Committee to contact the power company and negotiate an informal agreement to maintain water levels during the loon nesting season at a fairly constant level. It worked. Umbagog is now in the top three New Hampshire loon lakes for chick production.

Maine, too, has experienced problems with water fluctuations on some of its reservoirs, but according to Jane Arbuckle of the Maine Audubon Society, Maine utility officials have been cooperative by attempting to hold levels stable during the spring nesting season.

Harvest of Loons

In some parts of North America, loons are still used as a food source. Native Americans in Quebec kill an average of 4,500 loons each spring. Quebec fish and game officials estimate that the harvest is roughly twenty percent of the region's common loons, but add that it has not threatened the stability of the population. It is a small component of the Indian's diet, less than one-tenth of one percent according to a Quebec government report. In the far northwest, the Cree and Inuit have traditionally hunted loons, but the harvest now is thought to be slight.

While loons are not in a class with grain fed mallards, they should not be considered inedible. The early scientific literature has several references to the table quality of loons. One naturalist in the late 1800s termed loons "quite good," but few today are hungry enough to try one.

Predators

Faced with normal numbers of predators, loons do just

The damage raccoons can inflict on the loon population is well known. In New Hampshire they have been a particular nuisance. Like gulls, raccoons seem to be increasing in number throughout loon country. The feeding of raccoons by resort owners and tourists, coupled with the availability of garbage at land fills and waysides, has helped fuel the raccoon population expansion.

A Silver Lining

While this chapter presents a litany of problems, it does not translate into an epitaph for the loon. Though often costly, there are solutions to all of these challenges.

Sometimes a story is more appealing than its plot. The loon's story is part of a larger effort to put the world back together.

Gulls are a natural part of the northcountry but expanding populations might endanger loon productivity.   PHOTO BY WALT POMEROY

fine, but the populations of some predators, especially gulls and raccoons, have exploded in recent years, putting extra pressure on loon productivity. In Maine, gulls are a definite problem for loons. They take chicks, as well as eggs, often harass nesting loons, and sometimes take over prime nesting spots. Gulls are pretty, but they are also nasty. Niko Tinbergen, a Dutch naturalist, called gulleries "cities of thieves and murderers." To survive, gulls need to be aggressive. They will take whatever they can find, including loon eggs and chicks.

People Problems

"If lake residents are committed to preserving the primitive, pristine aspects of their lakes by protecting optimal nesting habitats for loons, then a comeback in loon populations can occur, and their presence will, in turn, enhance the lake's wild qualities."

—Scott Sutcliffe, 1980

Most loon problems are really people problems. Some, like chemical contamination, or excessive gull and raccoon populations, are camouflaged and removed by a layer or two from the core of loon problems—human ignorance and apathy. Other loon problems are all too visible: a loon with gunshot wounds, a loon with a hook deeply embedded in its gullet because a "sportsman" left a minnow unattended for hours, a loon entangled and immobilized by a plastic six-pack holder, a loon found dead from internal bleeding, the result of a let's-run-down-the-loon joyride. While all of these problems are real, they are fortunately rare. Aggressive public education efforts in most states have eliminated or at least reduced these excesses, but the quiet problems remain, like the nature photographer who must get a nesting loon shot and needs twelve attempts before getting the focus perfect.

Recreational Disturbance

The role of disturbance—intentional or unintentional— has been given considerable attention in loon management circles and has been frequently identified as the number-one threat to loon population stability. In nearly every state with a loon population, public education efforts have been mounted to prevent the disturbance of loons, especially during the nesting season. In Wisconsin, the line "Leave the Loons Alone" became the battle cry of loon protectionists with posters at boat landings, radio public service announcements, newspaper articles and campground slide programs all echoing the message. In New Hampshire, the issue was carried to its logical extreme. To protect loons from people, ropes with floats were strung across the mouths of bays or inlets to prevent boats from coming near a nest site. The rationale for this separation of loons and people was simple: boaters approaching the nest site dislodge the nesting bird and leave the eggs vulnerable to chilling or predation.

Recent loon research, however, questions the conventional wisdom. While it's certainly true that high levels of recreational activity near nest sites can affect hatching and chick rearing success, long-term recreational pressure is usually just one of many variables affecting productivity. The issue of recreational disturbance deserves a close review.

While loon researchers sounded the recreational alarm earlier, few people in wildlife management listened until non-game wildlife attracted the public's attention in the 1970s. A grass roots movement to stop harassment of loons began in New Hampshire in 1974 and quickly spread west.

Disturbing Research

Beginning in 1976 Jim Titus, who was completing his requirements for a Ph.D. at the State University of New York in Syracuse, conducted a detailed study of the impacts of recreation on loon productivity. Staking out the same study area that Sigurd Olson had used in 1950, Titus spent two full summers in the Boundary Waters Wilderness Area. With its loons, eagles, wolves, moose, northern lights, inspiring granite outcroppings, towering pines and over 1,000 lakes, the Boundary Waters is a magical place.

Titus claimed that the Boundary Waters Wilderness Area has "perhaps the largest and most concentrated contiguous breeding population of the common loon still remaining in any portion of the forty-eight adjoining states." When you add the million-plus acres and hundreds of lakes of Ontario's adjacent Quetico Provincial Park to the north, the many hundred lakes of the Superior National Forest to the south and the large loon lakes of Voyageurs National Park to the west, a picture of nearly perfect loon habitat emerges.

Studying all aspects of the disturbance question, Titus concluded that " . . . increased recreational use patterns had a negative effect on the productivity of the the common loon." He found that the heavy use of islands by campers offset the normal advantages of island nesting; that loons on small, remote lakes had a better hatching rate than those on large lakes in heavy recreation areas; that paddle-only (no motors allowed) lakes had better hatching and brooding success; and that where loons had fewer human contacts they produced more surviving young.

Comparing fifty nests in low-use areas with fifty nests in high-use areas, Titus found 0.61 juveniles per breeding pair surviving on low-use lakes and 0.43 surviving on high-use lakes. When he compared lakes where no motors were permitted, he found a similar difference; on paddle-only lakes the survival rate of juveniles per breeding pair was 0.71 compared to 0.50 on motor lakes. He reports in his dissertation that "pairs on non-motor lakes were consistently and significantly more successful in hatching young and raising broods."

The reason for these differences, Titus contended, is the loon pairs' attentiveness to nesting duties. When loons are defending their territory or hiding from human presence, they are obviously not on their nests and they expend considerable energy just avoiding people. (Judy McIntyre estimates that chicks facing heavy recreational pressures will expend up to eight times more energy than normal movements require.) When leaving a nest in a hurry, loons are not particularly careful. In his two-year study, Titus found eight intact loon eggs in the water near nests and suggested the hurried departure of disturbed birds was involved. Titus feels motors are a particular problem: "We had little doubt that the average party with motors on their craft affected the loons more than the average non-motor party." Forest Service biologist Catherine Ream also believed nest disturbance by canoeists was the primary limiting factor for loon reproduction in the Boundary Waters Wilderness Area.

By stepping back from the Titus and Ream studies and reviewing population trends for the area over a thirty-year period, a different perspective comes into focus. There is no question about the increase in recreational use of the Boundary Waters Wilderness Area: it was nearly ten times greater in 1984 than in 1950, when Sigurd T. Olson established a baseline estimate for loon population. Assuming that recreationists do disturb nesting birds, which in turn reduces productivity, a consistent decline in loon numbers would be expected. Such a decline has not occurred. With a survey completed in the summer of 1984, a thirty-four-year span of population estimates indicates that there were more loons and chicks in 1984 than in 1950, despite the tremendous increase in recreational use. Even though some loon nests in the Boundary Waters have been passed by 15,000 people per summer, loons have continued to successfully reproduce, although some territories have *moved* away from high use areas.

Learning to Cope?

This speaks well of the loon's tenacity and flexibility. It is quite possible, even likely, that loons have *learned* to tolerate human presence. Barrett Christenson, a graduate student from the University of Maine, studied nesting loons in 1979 and 1980 and concluded that "loons in Maine are habituating to disturbance by humans." He studied one group in a remote area of northern Maine and another in a heavily used area of southern Maine. While the birds in the remote areas quickly flushed when their nest was approached, the loons in southern Maine tended to sit tight when a boat came near. One particularly touchy pair of birds on Scraggly Lake in the northern study area flushed on thirty-seven of fifty approaches, even though the boat never came within a half-mile. A similar phenomenon was observed by Elizabeth Smith, a graduate student from Colorado State University, who studied common loons in Alaska. Working in the Kenai National Wildlife Refuge, she measured the average flushing distance on remote refuge lakes at about 350 feet. However, loons nesting along a heavily used refuge canoe route (2,500 canoes per summer) flushed at an average of just under thirty feet. Both these

An angler who left a minnow-baited rod unattended caught this immature loon which could not be saved.   PHOTO BY WILL MAINES/LAKELAND TIMES

X-ray shows embedded hook.

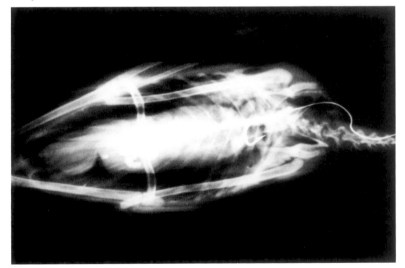

researchers concluded that loons simply get used to people.

Some loons carry this tolerance to an extreme. Titus discovered seven loons in his flock, all on high-use lakes, which refused to budge from their nests. Calling these birds "stickers", he found that even with approaches as close as three feet the birds never moved. In New Hampshire there are at least two loons whose mental glue to the nest was nothing short of bizarre. Scott Sutcliffe found two nesting loons, apparently in good health, so persistent in incubating that they had to be lifted off the nest to allow an egg count. Both birds were on busy lakes with heavy motorboat traffic. Another New Hampshire pair nested adjacent to a boathouse and actually swam through the boathouse to enter and leave the nest. Are these the last symbols of the wilderness we keep hearing about, or just smart loons?

There is a surprising twist to the disturbance story. In all studies, the birds on heavy-use lakes produced more chicks. The "stickers" on busy lakes produced far more chicks than loons on remote lakes. Two-chick broods were the norm for these tight-sitting birds. In a study of nesting success, Judy McIntyre found twenty-one of thirty-one loons (sixty-eight percent) nesting on high-use lakes were successful, while only thirteen of twenty-two loons (fifty-nine percent) nesting on low-use lakes were successful. Christenson's study in Maine demonstrated little difference in reproductive success. In the busy southern lakes twenty-one pair fledged fourteen young (0.67 per pair) while on the isolated northern lakes, fifteen pair fledged seven young (0.47 per pair). Christenson concluded that the "presence of people, cabins and human activity does not by itself appear to influence loon reproduction," but he did note that disturbances which keep birds off the nest for more than one hour are likely to cause nest abandonment.

So it's not just people—it's what they do and how long they do it. And it's not always a brash, insensitive fisherman who refuses to leave a nesting area. It can just as easily be the local naturalist in a cedar-strip Old Town with a Nikon who "needs" the ultimate loon photograph. People pressure does bother loons. The overlap of loon incubation and the prime fishing season may be a negative factor in loon productivity for some areas, and shore-to-shore boat traffic on Memorial Day or Independence Day certainly does not help. The success story of New Hampshire's loon protection effort clearly demonstrates the loon's need for separation from heavy recreational activity.

Certainly some human behaviors bother loons. I recall hearing loons on Trout Lake in northern Wisconsin start to call wildly on summer Sunday afternoons as soon as the weekly trapshoot began. Trout Lake resort owner Dan Cardinal told me the loons always react to the shooting. But the loons stay. They can tolerate disturbance and people, up to a point. Exactly where that point is will be the subject of discussion and debate for years—and maybe if we're lucky, forever.

Just like common loons, arctic loons like privacy near their nests.
PHOTO BY GARY JONES

Artificial nesting islands at times can bring common loons into areas where they will not be disturbed.
PHOTO BY TOM KLEIN

Since they nest only in the "far north" (above the tree line) yellow-billed loons are rarely bothered by recreationists.
PHOTO BY GARY JONES

The best strategy for a nesting loon is sitting tight. PHOTO BY GLENN IRWIN

Recovery Efforts

"Though the loon's breeding territory has shrunk dramatically, there is no reason that humans and loons can not share the same remaining northern waters, provided appropriate care is taken. It is the belief of The North American Loon Fund and the dedicated people who operate its programs that loons can not only survive in the modern world, but can thrive."

F or loons, the present is better than the past, and the future will be better than the present. The first half of that summary judgment on loons requires little supporting evidence. In the late nineteenth and early twentieth centuries, loon populations dwindled. At best, loons were considered a silly bird. At worse, they were seen as fishermen's competitors. Countless thousands were shot to protect fishermen's table fare. In the first quarter of the twentieth century, Edward H. Forbush documented an annual rite of spring when hundreds of loons were shot off Buzzards Bay in Massachusetts. In Maine, on postcard perfect Lake Umbagog, tourists shot loons for sport from cruise steamers. As late as the 1950s, loons served as targets on some Minnesota lakes.

Changing Attitudes

Carroll Henderson, the Minnesota DNR's Non-Game Coordinator, recalled at a 1981 Minneapolis loon confer-
ence that "sportsmen" in the late 1950s considered it their special responsibility to shoot all cormorants and loons on one western Minnesota lake. Henderson quickly noted that in a relatively short time people have come a long way; there are no more organized shoots for non-game water birds in Minnesota. Believing education programs about non-game wildlife are working, Henderson points to the recent re-establishment of white pelicans in Minnesota. Because their take of fish averages four pounds a day and their fishing technique is showy, even boisterous, fishermen despised the white pelican. By the late nineteenth century, these beautiful birds disappeared from Minnesota lakes—victims in a battle over fishing rights. The white pelican again nests on many Minnesota lakes and produces over a thousand young per summer. People are learning to live with predators, both feathered and furred. After years of expatriation, timber wolves have returned to northern Wisconsin's forests. And ospreys and bald eagles are expanding their range throughout the north. These are signs of the

times. Postive signs.

In the 1980s, loons are riding a high tide of good will. In New Hampshire, Rawson Wood has watched interest in loons grow tremendously over the past decade. He senses a deep emotional attachment between loons and New Hampshire's lake country residents and states the case quite graphically: "The Old Man of the Mountain is a beautiful part of New Hampshire. Anyone who destroyed it would probably be shot. Loons are a beautiful part of New Hampshire also. People feel strongly about loons. I don't think that will change."

Wood knows how deeply people in the East treasure the feeling of wilderness. He recalls the often quoted line from Edward Forbush's 1939 book, *The Natural History of Birds of Eastern and Central North America:* "Of all the wild creatures that persist in this region today, the loon seems best to typify the stark wilderness of primeval nature." Forbush was speaking of the Northeast in the early twentieth century.

His sentiment is echoed by many in the Northeast today. In New Hampshire and other areas of the East and Midwest, the loon is the only remaining symbol of wilderness. Rawson Wood estimates that few people in New Hampshire have ever seen an eagle, and ospreys are still rare. That makes loons all the more precious. In Wood's view, the future for loons depends upon how rapidly lakes are damaged by development, and how effectively people concerned with loons rally to protect them. With many other observers, he believes loons and people can live together, citing as proof recent productivity gains on New Hampshire lakes where heavy recreational pressure has been neutralized by aggressive public involvement and loon protection measures. He has watched with some pride the numbers of loons in New Hampshire increase from 254 in 1978 to 373 in 1984. The return of loons to Massachusetts is also encouraging to Wood and other North American Loon Fund officials. The first loon pair in years was spotted on the Quabbin Reservoir in 1975. By 1977 there were three pairs, and by 1984 there were five. Small numbers but in the right direction. Management programs have made these gains possible.

For centuries people have needed loons, but now, at least in some areas, loons need people, too. The *right* people. In New Hampshire, Jeff Fair of The Loon Preservation Committee considers public education and public involvement, his primary management tools, more important even than artificial nesting islands.

A Squam Lake resident for many years, Rawson Wood knows how important people are in the loon's future: "Loons can't possibly survive in New Hampshire without complete protection; the loon nests singly, in scattered locations, and can only be protected by the people who live on or visit its breeding lakes." In New Hampshire and in nearly every area where loons nest, loons are being well protected. Once common, harassment of loons by boaters is going the way of spring loon shoots. People are getting the message.

The Non-Game Movement

There is another reason for optimism: the non-game concept has spawned effective management programs in many states. As a result, the quality and quantity of loon research is increasing, and protection of shoreline breeding habitat in many areas is finally improving. Voluntary taxpayer contributions for non-game wildlife programs are helping loons in many states. Two examples: the Minnesota Non-Game Office in the Department of Natural Resources, supported by a non-game check-off, conducts an annual loon survey and sponsors important loon research; and the Wisconsin Department of Natural Resources' Non-Game Fund has assisted Wisconsin Project Loon Watch's vigorous public education effort. In New York and several other eastern states, loons are getting their share of the non-game pie.

In addition to education efforts, many state conservation agencies and private loon groups are protecting the loon's future prospects by placing artificial nesting islands in certain loon territories. Constructed of cedar logs, these islands are helping loon populations recover. In New Hampshire, over twenty percent of loon productivity is a direct result of their use. In the Chippewa National Forest in Minnesota, the use of artificial nest islands increased the nesting success rate on two lakes from twenty percent to seventy-one percent. By reducing the threat of predation (raccoons rarely swim to get eggs) and the possibilities of nest flooding or dry-docking (these islands float, adjusting to any lake level), artificial nesting islands work well. But they must be properly constructed and placed. Scott Sutcliffe offers a few tips: islands should be put in within two weeks of ice-out and be placed adjacent to previously used but unsuccessful sites where human disturbance will be minimal; islands should be protected from prevailing winds and located within 200 feet off shore in water ten to thirty feet deep; and the island should have a base of duff, twigs and roots with planted indigenous, low-lying vegetation.

Despite their success on many lakes, artificial islands are not a panacea for all the loon's troubles. A single nest island does not create ideal loon habitat. An adequate food supply, freedom from harassment and clean water are far more important than a mini swimming raft. Designed only to circumvent the effects of water level fluctuations and shoreline predation, articifical islands rarely attract new loons; they merely make successful nesting easier for loons already inhabiting an area. They are no more or less than temporary solutions for a very specific loon management problem.

The Big Picture

The major issues which threaten the loon's survival unfortunately cannot be solved with rafts, loon alert signs or loon bumper stickers. Even thousands of loon fanatics can not, by themselves, stop acid rain, toxic contamination or oil spills. Solutions in these areas await major legislative efforts which, in turn, await basic changes in societal values and priorities. But society continues to move in the direction of responsible environmental stewardship.

While political winds frequently change direction, creating setbacks, the progress in environmental protection over the past twenty years has been nothing short of remarkable.

Due in large part to the post-Earth Day surge of environmental legislation (especially The National Environmental Policy Act, The Clean Water Act, The Clean Air Act and The Endangered Species Act), environmental concerns in the United States have been institutionalized at nearly all levels of government. While the din of 1970s "rah-rah" environmentalism has faded, commitment to clean air and water, at personal and most governmental levels, has never been stronger. Aided by new pollution-control technologies and strong public support, emissions of acid-creating pollutants should decline by the turn of the twentieth century, in time to save the northern loon breeding lakes from acidification. That's a prediction based partly on knowledge and partly on faith. Its accuracy will depend, in part, on how effectively the conservation community addresses the economic questions related to acid rain control measures.

The challenges of cleaning up toxic contaminants and heavy metals such as lead, mercury and aluminum will probably be more demanding. The sources of these contaminants are usually diffuse: an insecticide sprayed on southern agricultural lands can be carried in the atmosphere to loon lakes in Wisconsin or Maine. While DDT or PCBs do not appear to be a present threat to loons, other potentially harmful chemicals could be patiently waiting in the food chain. At a 1984 conference, sponsored by the Sigurd Olson Environmental Institute of Northland College, Valdas Adamkus underscored this point. The U.S. Environmental Protection Agency Administrator for the Great Lakes

PHOTO BY WOODY HAGGE

region, Adamkus told conference participants that over 200 man-made compounds have been found in Great Lakes predator fish which feed at the top of the food chain. Even more disturbing for the audience was the statement by Adamkus that "Our knowledge of nearly all of these compounds is limited . . . for most of them, health-effects information simply does not exist."

Information specific to the effects of various contaminants on loons is slim, although it appears loons cope fairly well with some contaminants. One does not have to be a scientist to see some of the effects of chemical contamination in waterbirds. High levels of toxicants in Lake Michigan's Green Bay, for example, have affected cormorants and four other bird species by causing gross bill deformities. Unable to feed efficiently, such birds are doomed, the victims most likely of dioxin.

At a public hearing in Green Bay, Wisconsin on Senator Robert Kasten's "Save the Lakes" bill, a pair of these cormorants were on display. Looking at these birds elicited simultaneous feelings of revulsion and fascination. Were they just a cruel joke of nature, or an apocalyptic symbol of an unwanted future? The toxic contamination issue represents a serious challenge for the research community, government agencies, environmental groups and concerned citizens. Those cormorants do not have to represent the future of wildlife. With the proper blend of research, new technology, persuasion and patience, the toxic issue can be satisfactorily resolved.

The Adaptable Loon

Patience is something loons probably know a lot about. Over hundreds of thousands of years, loons have adjusted to a broad range of environmental change. Unlike people, loons and all other wildlife species don't worry about change; they simply adapt to it or perish. Succeeding in a variety of habitats and adjusting nesting habits to minimize human

Cross-billed deformities in cormorants and other species are abnormally frequent in the Green Bay area. Toxic contaminants are responsible.
PHOTO BY TIM KUBIAK

interference, loon behavior is quite elastic. Most likely, loons will not replay the sad story of the ivory-billed woodpecker. This large woodpecker was widely distributed in the virgin forests of southern North America until the logging of mature forests destroyed its preferred habitat. Today the existence of the ivory-billed is limited to rumors and hoaxes.

The loon's path will probably be closer to the one followed by the pileated woodpecker, which shared the ivory-billed's habitat and food supply. For reasons not well understood, the pileated woodpecker could adapt to changing environmental conditions; it survived and thrived in younger growth woodlands. While not as common as crows, pileated woodpeckers are turning up all over. Their flexible feeding habits gave pileated woodpeckers a second chance; the rigid patterns of the ivory-billed gave that bird a one-way ticket to oblivion.

Loons seem to be anything but rigid: they nest on a wide variety of lakes from one acre to thousands of acres in size; they construct their nests out of any available material; they eat almost anything aquatic; and in winter they disperse over an enormous coastal range. It seems like an open-ended ticket. Even if acid rain were to wipe out the trout or smallmouth bass of a given region, loons would simply feed more heavily on perch or suckers, more resistant prey species. Loons have more time than many other members of the lake community to ride out the acid rain threat.

It also seems that loons can live with people. The stability of the loon population in the Boundary Waters Wilderness Area, despite twenty years of rapidly increasing recreational use, is strong evidence for believing loons and people can co-exist.

While there still are serious problems in the current reproductive success of loons, especially in the Northeast, these problems can probably be solved through protection and management efforts. Dominated by enormous numbers of loons breeding in Canada, the total North American population appears adequate to feed a recovery effort as suitable loon habitat becomes available. In Wisconsin, after generations of inching northward, the range of breeding loons is starting to reverse directions and move to the south. Improved water quality, resulting from a decade of tough enforcement of the Clean Water Act, and a reduction of harassment are part of that change.

There is hope that loons in Wisconsin and elsewhere can reoccupy parts of their traditional breeding range. To some, that may seem unrealistic, even miraculous. But look at some other modern environmental miracles: Lake Erie, returned from the "dead," producing some of the best walleye fishing in the world; the Connecticut River again producing Atlantic salmon; peregrine falcons now expanding their endangered population; and the whooping crane, once a lonely group of eighteen birds and written off by many biologists, slowly moving back from the brink of extinction as a band of eighty-four wild and sixty-five captive birds. We're not about to write off the common loon.

Hope

I often receive notes from some of Wisconsin Project Loon Watch's 700 volunteer cooperators citing the failure of a loon pair to successfully hatch a chick. Sometimes these cooperators assume personal responsibility for a loon's failure and they always use the occasion to lament about the future of loons on their lake. I usually return a note of appreciation for their concern, but remind them that loons are long-lived birds, that adult mortality of loons is relatively low and that it takes only two surviving chicks over the pair's entire life span to continue the species.

Despite the insults of water pollution, harassment and habitat loss, the population of the common loon has declined only slightly over the past thirty years, and in some parts of its range breeding populations have actually started to climb slightly. Research is expanding in a variety of areas critical for improved loon management, and new tools for research such as the audiospectrograph and radio-tracking equipment are becoming available. In July of 1984, a bald eagle was tracked by an orbiting satellite, opening a new era in telemetry research. In the twenty-first century, loons fitted with transmitters will probably be routinely followed by satellite from their northern summer homes to warm coastal waters.

All loons ask for is a place to live, clean water, some fish to eat and a little privacy. For what loons give to people, that seems a small price to pay.

Sources

Loon Lover's Digest

"The loons are flying above us, still laughing. I would like to laugh as jubilantly."
—*Florence Page Jaques, 1938*

After nearly a decade of giving loon lectures, I think I've heard just about every conceivable question about loons. All of the following have surfaced at public programs, most given in northern Wisconsin. A couple of the trickier ones, though, came from the 1984 New Hampshire Loon Festival and the 1985 Maine Loon Festival.

The questions are arranged by level of fanaticism: the early ones are the predictable, get 'em at every Rotary or Kiwanis luncheon; the middle ones are heard less frequently, but occasionally at something like a regional Audubon conference; the last dozen or so questions are special, the products of minds with too much free time over the long northern winters. You will know them when you see them.

Fifty Questions About Loons
The Top Ten: For All Loon Lovers

1. *Do loons mate for life?*

   The heart says "yes," but the head says "maybe." There simply isn't enough information to answer this one. Since the pair bond isn't strong enough to keep the loon pair together throughout migration and wintering, it may not be strong enough to insure a lifelong partnership. There appears to be, however, a strong fidelity to the nest site. A loon pair probably returns to the same territory and nest site. If a member of a pair dies, the other will most likely find a new mate.

2. *Why is the eye red?*

   Many scientists believe that the red eye improves fishing abilities either by improved underwater vision or by its camouflage effect (the red eye appears gray at depths of fifteen feet or more).

3. *How can you tell the difference between males and females?*

   It's not easy. You can wait for one to lay an egg (that's a female), watch a pair copulate (the male is on top) or notice which bird gives the distinctive yodel call (only males give this call). There are no differences in plumage and only slight differences in size.

4. *How long do loons live?*

   Most scientists believe the average life expectancy to be fifteen to thirty years.

5. *Just how ancient is the loon?*

   It is no accident that loons are listed first in bird books. They are the oldest living birds with an ancestry dating back fifty to eighty million years. The oldest loon fossils date back twenty million years.

6. *How did the loon get its common name?*

   This is a multiple choice question. Most reference books relate the common loon to the English word *lumme* or the Scandinavian word *lom*, both meaning awkward or lame. Since the loon is very clumsy on land, these references do make sense.

   The *Oxford Book of British Bird Names*, published in late 1984, suggests the word loon was a seventeenth century corruption of the Old Norse word *lómr* which referred to the red-throated loon. The basic meaning of the Norse word is moaning, an allusion to the loud, wailing calls of the loon. In the seventeenth century loon meant "a fool." Shakespeare's Macbeth called a servant "a cream-faced loon" which one Shakespearian scholar translated as "stupid fellow."

7. *Do loons use their wings while diving?*

   No. The wings are used to help execute sharp turns while chasing prey, but they are not used for propulsion. The large webbed feet supply the power. Wings are typically held tight to the body during dives.

8. *How deep do loons dive?*

   There are reports of dives in excess of 200 feet, but no scientific evidence exists for dives to those depths. It's safe to say loons dive to depths over 100 feet which is amazing enough anyway. Generally loons fish in shallow water and stay submerged less than one minute.

9. *Are loons endangered?*

   Officially the answer is no. Common loons are not on the U.S. Fish and Wildlife's List of Endangered or Threatened Species. In some parts of their range, however, the common loon is in trouble. Many states list the loon as endangered, rare or threatened.

10. *How fast do loons fly?*

    Loons have been clocked at speeds over 100 mph. Having wing beats of around 250 per minute, the common loon is an extremely rapid flyer considering its adaptations (solid bones for example) which favor aquatic over aerial freedom.

The Next Ten: For Serious Loon Watchers

11. *What's the wild calling at night all about?*

The extravagant calling at night is probably part of territorial defense. Loons like to keep track of each other. In daylight they can see each other, but at night they have only calling. Termed night chorusing, this calling peaks in early spring and has to be considered as one of nature's most exciting audio events.

12. *How large are loon territories?*

Territory size will depend upon the quality of habitat and the density of loons in the region, but twenty to 100 acres covers the range. In prime northern Minnesota loon country, the average territory on large lakes is about seventy acres.

13. *How many species of loons are there?*

A very small family, there are only four species of loons—the common, the red-throated, the arctic and the yellow-billed. There are no subspecies of loons.

14. *How large are loons?*

Common loons average around ten pounds. There is a size gradient. Loons from the northeast are larger (averaging about twelve pounds) than loons from the upper midwest (averaging about nine pounds). The typical loon is about thirty inches in length with a wingspread of fifty inches.

15. *What's the ideal nest site?*

Imagine a spot right next to the water on the protected side of a small island with plenty of low vegetation. Have the water drop off quickly to a depth of around five feet. Now you have a picture of a perfect loon nest site. If your lake has only one small island, odds are high that your loons will be nesting there.

16. *What does courtship activity look like?*

There will never be an X-rated loon movie. Loon courtship is rather mild: combinations of short dives, bill dipping and bill flicking while quietly swimming near the shoreline.

17. *Who builds the nest?*

Loons have been liberated for millions of years. Males and females divide about equally the nest building duties. Loons are not careful builders. They simply throw whatever vegetation is handy on the nest.

18. *About the eggs, how many and how big?*

Loons aren't like ducks which lay clutches of a dozen or more eggs. Generally, loons lay two eggs, sometimes only one and very rarely three. Of course if ducks laid eggs which averaged 3⅜" in length and 2¼" in diameter, they would not lay a dozen either. Loons incubate their eggs an average of twenty-eight days, but successful incubation can be as short as twenty-five or as long as thirty-three days. The eggs are turned (very carefully) with the loon's open mandibles at irregular intervals.

19. *What predators go after loon eggs?*

The masked bandit (raccoon) we all know and love is presently loon enemy #1. Primarily nocturnal, raccoons are aggressive enough and large enough to barge into a mainland loon nest, chase away the adult and feast on loon eggs. In 1975, before New Hampshire's loon

rangers started using artificial nest islands (raccoons can, of course, swim but they rarely bother loons on islands), raccoons destroyed up to eighty percent of all loon eggs on some New Hampshire lakes. Raccoons, though, tend to be a problem only where people with their garbage have inflated raccoon populations. In wilderness areas, avian predators such as ravens or crows probably take more eggs than mammals.

20. *Are loon eggshells getting thin?*

Pesticides, especially DDT, have created problems for many birds. While eagles, ospreys and peregrines have suffered from eggshell thinning, though, loons have continued to successfully reproduce. Loon eggshells are about ten percent thinner than eggshells from the pre-DDT era.

Ten More: Casual Readers Beware

21. *If the egg hatches, what are the odds the chick will survive?*

Very good. Since the parental care of chicks is excellent (by human standards, obsessive), adult loons usually see their chick(s) through to fall migration. One New Hampshire study determined that eight-four percent of all hatched chicks survived.

22. *What time of year gives loons the most trouble?*

It's certainly not summer when loons enjoy a season of easy fishing and slight stress. Very few dead adult loons are found on northern lakes. Disease often affects loons in the fall when large numbers congregate: thousands of loons have succumbed to botulism on Lake Michigan. But winter is the loon's worst season. The stress of coping with salt water, violent winter storms, marine pollution and parasites make life on the coast tough for loons. Off the coasts of the Carolinas, Florida or Texas, natural selection does its best work.

23. *How often do loons come ashore?*

Usually only to nest. A loon is a total water bird. It is not inconceivable that a loon (if it did not mate) could live out its entire life without placing a foot on terra firma.

24. *Can loons walk?*

Not really. Loons sort of push themselves along on land but cannot stand erect and walk like a duck or goose. The legs are simply too far back on the body. Ninety-nine percent of all the mounted specimens are lies, showing loons standing up straight on their two huge feet.

25. *What do loons eat?*

Mainly fish. If a loon lives on a lake with an abundant fish population, the loon will probably eat fish ninety-nine percent of the time. Favored prey are perch, suckers, bullheads, sunfish, smelt and minnows. Non-fish items on the menu include frogs, salamanders, crayfish and leeches. Keep in mind that loons are very flexible feeders: they eat what they find.

26. *Do loons eat game fish?*

Sure. They love trout if they can find them. Small northern pike, bass or walleye all look the same to a hungry loon. Unlike people, loons don't distinguish between game fish and rough fish—a meal is a meal.

PHOTO BY GLENN IRWIN

27. *What about salt water diets?*

Fewer studies of salt water feeding habits have been done but it's safe to say loons use the same opportunistic fishing strategies there. Herring, sea trout, rock cod, flounder would certainly be on the menu.

28. *How big a fish can a loon handle?*

Since loons have a rather elastic esophagus, they can swallow fairly large prey including trout up to eighteen inches. Spiny prey like sunfish or walleye may present a problem. Loons have been found dead with two pound walleyes stuck in their gullets. Such large prey, however, are the exception: the average loon prey can be weighed in ounces rather than pounds.

29. *What is the "penguin dance?"*

Well named, the loon's penguin dance is the bird's most dramatic territorial display. Loons literally stand on the water by violently kicking their feet. While this defensive display might drive away some natural enemies, it does not work well with people. Some uninformed fishermen or boaters think it's entertainment and stimulate the display. It requires a lot of energy to perform (try it next time you're swimming). Anyone accidently stimulating the dance should retreat immediately.

The Thirties: Fanatics Only

30. *Why do chicks climb on their parent's back?*

The back-riding of chicks is primarily to protect against heat loss but also serves as protection from underwater (snapping turtles or pike) or overwater (eagles) predators.

31. *How high can loons fly?*

According to information from radar, at least 7,000 feet. Most flights in summer are at altitudes of only several hundred feet.

32. *Can loons lay more than one set of eggs a season?*

Yes, if their eggs are lost to predators, loons will lay another clutch of eggs. Sometimes loons will even nest a third time if the second batch of eggs is lost.

33. *Do loons have a "brood patch?"*

While loons do not have a featherless brood patch (an incubation hot spot), they do have an area of their breast where blood vessels in the skin increase in size during the roughly one-month incubation period. This physiological change better transfers the bird's body heat to the eggs.

34. *What does the "wing flap" signify?*

The "wing flap" is done by many water birds. It probably has no social significance and is simply a way to shake water out of feathers.

35. *Why don't loons nest every year?*

Being a long-lived bird with the potential to raise dozens of young, loons don't need to attempt a nest each year. If the conditions aren't quite right, they often forego nesting. Typically, loons nest three of every four years.

36. *What is a "rogue loon?"*

The term has been given to non-territorial birds or un-successful parents that wander around lakes in late summer. Occasionally, they kill other loons' chicks. This is not unusual behavior in the animal kingdom. Young, unattended birds and mammals are often killed by non-parent adults.

37. *Do loons have accents?*

No. Loons from Minnesota sound just like loons from Maine or New Hampshire.

38. *Will loon eggs die if the nest is left uncovered?*

Loon eggs are susceptible to cooling. If left uncovered for long periods, the embryo could die. However, on hot days an egg might survive six or eight hours without incubation. Typically large eggs hold heat better than small eggs so loon eggs are better protected than the eggs of most birds.

39. *Why do some loons tolerate people better than others?*

It appears that loons habituate to people over time. Apparently each loon has individual characteristics regarding tolerance of disturbance.

The Final Ten: Beyond Fanaticism

40. *Do some loons have green heads?*

Looks are deceiving. A loon's head sometimes looks green but it's really jet-black. When the feathers on the head are slightly raised (a display loons use in social gatherings) sunlight refracting through the feathers creates the green, iridescent effect. In an argument, bet on black.

41. *Do loons nest on the ocean?*

No. There has never been a report of a loon nesting on the coast. However, loons are commonly seen off the coasts of Maine and New Hampshire during the summer breeding season. These birds are either travelers from inland lakes or single loons unable to find fresh-water breeding territories.

42. *Okay, what is this foot waggle business?*

All serious loon watchers know about the foot waggle. Every ten to twenty minutes loons will extend a foot and wave it. It could be that the foot is being used as a crude solar collector to pick up heat. The waggle certainly conserves heat since the blood vessels in the foot would release heat to the water. Supporting this notion is the fact that after the waggle, the foot is usually tucked up under the wing—a place to keep it warm. Or it could be that the foot waggle is part of a stretching exercise, loon yoga perhaps.

43. *Are small lakes better habitat for loons than large lakes?*

Small lakes are probably better habitat for loons, especially if one pair is able to claim the entire lake as its territory. This reduces competition for food and other resources and allows the loons to focus all of their attention on raising their young. Chicks may actually develop more rapidly on small ponds than on large lakes.

44. *When does the molt begin?*

The fall molt seems to vary by region—earlier in the west and later in the east. The first noticeable loss of feathers is usually mid-to-late September. New breeding plumage is donned in March and April. Loons lose their wing feathers only once—in late winter, usually February.

45. *In summer, do loons travel much?*

Recent research indicates loons travel a lot in summer, especially late summer after nesting duties are completed. One Wisconsin loon, tracked with a radio transmitter, flew twelve miles from its home lake to feed in another lake.

46. *How many loons have been banded?*

Five-hundred and eighty-seven. Next question. . .

47. *How old are loons before they return to the northern lakes?*

Unlike ducks or geese, loons hang around their coastal homes for a full two or even three years before reaching sexual maturity and flying north for the first time. These immature loons do not have the black and white plumage. This delayed breeding might give loons the time they need to learn the fishing and general survival skills necessary to successfully raise young.

48. *Will loons reject a chick touched by humans?*

No. Many chicks have been handled for banding and have been safely returned to their parents. Other chicks, which were abandoned, have been rescued by people and subsequently adopted by adult loons.

49. *How long after copulation will the eggs be laid?*

That's a rather personal question and no biologist seems to have the answer. It is a short period of time though, measured in days rather than weeks.

50. *Where do I find out even more about loons?*

You are an over-the-edge loon fanatic. But if you want information on loons in your region, contact the North American Loon Fund affiliate closest to you.

North American Loon Fund
Main St., Humiston Building
Meredith, New Hampshire 03853
603/279-6163

Affiliated Loon Groups

Common Loon Protection Project
Maine Audubon Society
118 Old Route 1
Falmouth, ME 04105

Loon Survey Project
Vermont Institute of Natural Science
Woodstock, VT 05091

Loon Preservation Committee
Audubon Society of New Hampshire
Main Street
Meredith, NH 03253

Minnesota Loon Appreciation Committee
812 Oriole Lane
Chaska, MN 55318

Loon Project
Adirondack Council
P.O. Box D2
Elizabethtown, NY 12932

Wisconsin Project Loon Watch
Sigurd Olson Environmental Institute
Northland College
Ashland, Wisconsin 54806

Ontario Lakes Loon Survey
Long Point Bird Observatory
P.O. Box 160
Port Rowan, Ontario
NOE 1MO

Common Loon Summary

Age (Individuals)—15 to 30 years.

Age (Species)—Oldest and most primitive living bird, at least 20 million years old.

Autumn Migration—October and November; Pre-migratory flocking occurs on staging lakes; Flight groups usually small.

Chicks—12–24 Hours: Leave nest with adult.
First Day: make shallow dives.
First Week: begin diving for food.
First Month: dependent on adults for food.
6 Weeks: reach adult size.
6–8 Weeks: attain self-sufficiency.
11 Weeks: initial flight, possible dispersion.

Copulation—Normally occurs on land near nest site.

Courtship—Gentle, ritualized bill-dipping, shallow dives and head rubbing.

Diet—Mainly fish but also frogs, salamanders, crayfish, leeches, and aquatic greens. Loons feed by sight, grasp prey with their bills (they do *not* spear prey), and swallow most prey underwater.

Dives—Depth, perhaps to 200 feet; Duration, up to 5 minutes but generally under 1 minute; Loons are quick and mobile underwater.

Eggs—Loons typically lay two large eggs one day apart, olive green-brown with dark brown spots, 3⅜ inches long, 2¼ inches in diameter.

Flight—Runway, ⅛ mile or less; Air Speed, 75–100 mph.

Incubation—Shared by both males and females for 27 to 31 days (average 28 days).

Molting—Flight feathers, once each year during late winter: Breast and back feathers, twice each year, October–December and again during March–April.

Nest Construction—Pile of mud and available vegetation with shallow depression in middle; Additional construction and repairs made during incubation.

Nest Sites—Island locations preferred near water's edge and protected from prevailing winds; Some well camouflaged, others exposed.

Physical Description—Male and female identically colored.
Summer Plumage: glossy black head, black neck with white and black necklace around throat, checkered black and white back and wings, white underparts; straight and black bill; eyes, deep red.
Winter Plumage: dark gray-brown head, neck and back, white throat and underparts.

Predators (chicks)—Large fish, snapping turtles and eagles.

Predators (eggs)—Raccoons, gulls, crows, ravens, skunks, minks and otters.

Range—Summer Nesting Grounds: Canada, Alaska, Iceland, Greenland, and northern United States (ME, NH, VT, NY, MI, WI, MN).
Wintering Grounds: Atlantic coast from Maine to Florida Keys, Gulf of Mexico from Florida to Texas, Pacific coast from California Baja to southern Alaska.

Scientific Name—Gavia immer

Sexual Maturity—3 years for loons to reach maturity.

Size—Length, 28 to 35 inches; Weight, 8 to 12 pounds; Wingspan, up to 58 inches; Males slightly larger than females.

Spring Migration—April and May; Males arrive within a few days of ice out; Females arrive a few days or a week after the male's arrival.

Origins

"No one is so well aware of the many shortcomings and omissions in this work as the author. If the reader fails to find mentioned in these pages some things which he knows about the birds, he can blame himself for not having sent them to the author."
—*Arthur Cleveland Bent, 1919*

Whttp://when Bent wrote his *Life Histories of North American Diving Birds* in 1919, the fraternity of bird lovers and potential readers was limited. Not so today. I blame only myself for any omissions. Bent, of course, did not have the benefits of computer literature searches, nor the sixty-five years of loon research which followed his publication.

While I did not count each page, I did estimate the volume of technical papers about loons at 4,000 pages. The *Selected Bibliography* in this section, organized by topical areas, is the tip of the iceberg.

If you want more information but don't like chipping away at icebergs, try the *Proceedings of the Second North American Conference on Common Loon Research and Management*, available through North American Loon Fund, the section on loons in *The Audubon Society Encyclopedia of North American Birds* or the first chapter of R. S. Palmer's *Handbook of North American Birds.*

Published materials, however, give only part of the loon's story. Many areas of research, especially population estimates, never see the printed page. A telephone is often the best research tool. While over a hundred persons were contacted during the research phase of this book, fifty people provided valuable information and deserve recognition:

Valdas Adamkus, Environmental Protection Agency
Ray Anderson, University of Wisconsin-Stevens Point
Joe Anderlik, amateur loon watcher
Jane Arbuckle, Maine Audubon Society
Paul Arneson, Alaska Fish and Game Commission
Delores Bainbridge, Native American historian
John Bissonette, U.S. Fish and Wildlife
Mark Blackbourn, Northwoods Wildlife Center
Christopher Brand, U.S. Fish and Wildlife
Peter Croskery, Ontario Ministry of Natural Resources
David Ewert, Iowa Nature Conservancy
Jeff Fair, New Hampshire Loon Preservation Committee
Donald Forrester, University of Florida
Dan Gibson, University of Alaska Museum
John Gustafson, California Dept. of Fish and Game
Woody Hagge, loon photographer

Paul Hansen, Izaak Walton League
Dan Helwig, Minnesota Pollution Control Agency
Carroll Henderson, Minnesota Dept. of Nat. Resources
Joseph Hickey, University of Wisconsin-Madison
Dale Hjertaas, Saskatchewan Parks Department
David Hussell, Ontario Ministry of Natural Resources
Glenn Irwin, loon photographer
Grace James, amateur loon watcher
James King, U.S. Fish and Wildlife (retired)
Randy Kreil, North Dakota Natural Heritage Inventory
Tim Kubiack, U.S. Fish and Wildlife
Robert Lange, U.S. Fish and Wildlife
John Lerg, Michigan Department of Natural Resources
Harry Lumsten, Ontario Ministry of Natural Resources
Kelly McAllister, Washington Dept. of Fish and Game
Guy McCashie, *American Birds*, California
Ed Miller, Governors State University
Keewaydinoquay, University of Wisconsin-Milwaukee
David Moore, Alberta Natural Resources Ministry
Denny Olson, Sigurd Olson Environmental Institute
John Olson, Wisconsin Department of Natural Resources
Sigurd T. Olson, loon researcher
Jim Pierce, Wisconsin Project Loon Watch
Richard Plunkett, North American Loon Fund
Mark Schaefer, U.S. Fish and Wildlife
Dave Sheppard, Long Point Bird Observatory
Malcolm Simons, Atlantic Beached Bird Survey
Dan Small, Northland College
Ken Sorlien, amateur loon watcher
Paul Strong, University of Maine-Orono
Sylvia Taylor, Michigan Department of Natural Resources
Steve Thompson, Nisqually Wildlife Refuge
Rawson Wood, North American Loon Fund
Gary Zimmer, Wisconsin Project Loon Watch

The Images

Loon photography is complicated by several factors: most loons are elusive and quite shy; all loons except nesting birds, move around a lot and loons, of course, are on or near water making exposures tricky. The images of *Loon Magic* are the products of an extensive, continent-wide search. Over fifty professional and many more amateur wildlife photographers were contacted. Surprisingly few had quality loon photographs.

Without question Woody Hagge, based near the heart of northern Wisconsin's loon country, had the finest collection* of loon material. His material covered beautifully the nesting, chick rearing and feeding activities.

Another Wisconsin photographer, retired physician Glenn Irwin, had a series of exceptionally sharp nesting shots. Glenn spent several summers getting to know his favorite subject, a loon called Maggie.

Based in Ely, Minnesota at the doorstep of the Quetico-Superior canoe country, biologist/photographer Lynn Rogers had the patience to capture the once-in-a-lifetime photograph of a just hatched chick (see page x.).

Dave Repp, an Indiana photographer in love with the north country, had the foresight to bring some film on a couple of early fall canoe trips in the Boundary Waters Wilderness and returned with beautiful shots of feeding, flying and molting loons.

Other important visual contributors included Tom Mangelsen, Edgar Jones and Stephen Krasemann.

*Most of the Hagge photographs in *Loon Magic* are available as notecards or prints. Contact Woody Hagge at Loonar Enterprises, Inc., P.O. Box 10, Hazelhurst, Wisconsin 54531 for details.

PHOTOS BY WOODY HAGGE

Selected Bibliography

Nesting and Chick Rearing

Beebe, C. William, "Notes on the Early Life of Loon Chicks," *Auk*, Vol. 24, pp. 34-41, 1907.

Johnson, R. A. and Hazel, "A Study of the Nesting and Family Life of the Red-throated Loon," *Wilson Bulletin*, Vol. 47, pp. 97-103, 1935.

Mathisen, John and J. M., "Artificial Islands as Nest Sites for Common Loons," *Journal of Wildlife Management*, Vol. 41 (2), pp. 317-319, 1977.

Munro, J. A., "Observations of the Loon in the Caribou Packlands, British Columbia," *Auk*, Vol. 62, pp. 38-49, 1945.

McIntyre, Judith, "Nurseries: A Consideration of Habitat Requirements During the Early Chick-Rearing Period in Common Loons," *Journal of Field Ornithology*, Vol. 54, pp. 247-253, 1983.

Biology and Behavior of the Common Loon "Gavia Immer" With Reference to Its Adaptability in a Man-Altered Environment, Ph.D. Thesis, University of Minnesota, 1975.

Olson, Sigurd T., *A Study of the Common Loon in the Superior National Forest of Northern Minnesota*, Master's Thesis, University of Minnesota, 1951.

Peterson, Margaret R., "Nesting Ecology of Arctic Loons," *Wilson Bulletin*, Vol. 91, pp. 608-617, 1979.

Sjolander, Sverre and Agren, Greta, "Reproductive Behavior of the Common Loon," *Wilson Bulletin*, Vol. 84, pp. 296-308, 1972.

"Reproductive Behavior of the Yellow-billed Loon, Gavia adamsii," *The Condor*, Vol. 78, pp. 454-463, 1976.

Southern, W. E., "Copulatory Behavior of the Common Loon", *Wilson Bulletin*, Vol. 73, p. 280, 1961.

Sutcliffe, Scott A., *Aspects of the Nesting Ecology of the Common Loon in New Hampshire*, Master's Thesis, University of New Hampshire, 1980.

"Changes in Status: Factors Affecting Common Loon Populations in New Hampshire," *Trans. of the Northeast Section of the Wildlife Society*, 35th Northeast Fish and Wildlife Conference, pp. 219-244, 1978.

"Artificial Common Loon Nesting Site Construction, Placement and Utilization in New Hampshire," The New Hampshire Loon Preservation Committee, Meredith, New Hampshire, 1979.

Tate, James and Jean, "Mating Behavior of the Common Loon," *Auk*, Vol. 87, pp. 125-130, 1970.

Vermeer, Kees, "Some Aspects of the Nesting Requirement of Common Loons in Alberta," *Wilson Bulletin*, Vol. 85, pp. 429-435, 1973.

Distribution

Armstrong, Robert H., *A Guide to the Birds of Alaska*, Alaska Northwest Publishing Co., Anchorage, Alaska, 1980.

Baily, Alfred M., *Birds of Arctic Alaska*, Colorado Museum of Natural History, 1948.

Desgranges, Jean-Luc, "Preliminary Consideration of the Status of Loons in Quebec," Canadian Wildlife Service, Quebec Region, 1979.

Godfrey, William E., *Birds of Canada*, National Museum of Canada Bulletin 203, Ottawa, 1966.

Henderson, A.D., "The Common Loon in Alberta," *The Condor*, Vol. 26, pp. 143-145, 1924.

Hollister, N. and Kumlien, L., *The Birds of Wisconsin*, Wisconsin Natural History Society, Milwaukee, 1903.

Ridgeway, Robert, *The Ornithology of Illinois*, Vol. II, State Legislature of Illinois, 1895.

Roberts, Thomas S., *The Birds of Minnesota*, University of Minnesota Press, 1932.

Sage, Bryan, "A Study of White-billed Divers in Arctic Alaska," *British Birds*, Vol. 64, pp. 519-527, 1971.

Synder, L. L., *Ontario Birds*, Clarke, Irwin & Co., Toronto, 1951.

Zimmer, Gary, "Status of the Common Loon in Wisconsin," Wisconsin Department of Natural Resources, 1978.

Human Disturbance

Christenson, Barrett L., *Reproductive Ecology and Response to Disturbance by Common Loons in Maine*, Master's Thesis, University of Maine, Orono, 1981.

Ream, Catherine, "Loon Productivity: Human Disturbance and Pesticide Residue in Northern Minnesota," *Wilson Bulletin*, Vol. 88, pp. 426-431, 1976.

Smith, Elizabeth L., *Effects of Canoeing on Common Loon Production and Survival on the Kenai National Wildlife Refuge*, Master's Thesis, Colorado State University, 1981.

Titus, James R., *Response of the Common Loon "Gavia Immer" to Recreational Pressure in the Boundary Waters Canoe Area*, Ph.D. Thesis, State University of New York, Syracuse, N.Y., 1977.

Behavior

Able, Kenneth, "Studying Migration," *Birdwatchers Digest*, Vol. 7, No. 1, 1984.

Barklow, William E., *The Function of Variations in the Vocalizations of the Common Loon (Gavia Immer)*, Ph.D. Thesis, Tufts University, 1979.

Ewert, David N., "Spring Migration of Loons at Whitefish Point, Michigan," *The Jack Pine Warbler*, Vol. 60, No. 4, 1982.

"The Wildest Calling," *Michigan Natural Resources*, June, 1983.

Flick, William A., "Observations on Loons as Predators on Brook Trout", *North American Journal of Fisheries Management*, Vol. 3, pp. 95-96, 1983.

Goetzinger, Charles and Rummel, Lynda, "The Communication of Intraspecific Aggression in the Common Loon," *Auk*, Vol. 92, pp. 333-346, 1975.

PHOTO BY R. C. BURKE

Sources

"Aggressive Display in the Common Loon," *Auk*, Vol. 95, pp. 183-186, 1978.

King, Bernard, "Wintering Feeding Behavior of Great Northern Divers," *British Birds*, Vol. 69, p. 468, 1966.

McIntyre, Judith, "Wintering Behavior of the Common Loon," *Auk*, Vol. 95, pp. 396-403, 1978.

"Pre-migratory Behavior of Common Loons on the Autumn Staging Grounds," *Wilson Bulletin*, Vol. 95, pp. 121-125, 1983.

Biology and Behavior of the Common Loon "Gavia Immer" With Reference to Its Adaptability in a Man-Altered Environment, Ph.D. Thesis, University of Minnesota, 1975.

Norberg, J. M. and R. A., "Take-off, Landing and Flight Speed During Fishing Flights of Gavia stellata," *Ornis. Scand.*, Vol. 2, pp. 55-67, 1971.

Norton, Arthur, "The Loon," Educational Leaflet No. 78, The National Association of Audubon Societies, 1928.

Olson, Sigurd T., *A Study of the Common Loon in the Superior National Forest of Northern Minnesota*, Master's Thesis, University of Minnesota, 1951.

Pittman, James A., "Direct Observation of Flight Speed of the Common Loon," *Wilson Bulletin*, Vol. 65, p. 213, 1953.

Schorger, A. W., "The Deep Diving of the Loon and Old-Squaw and its Mechanisms," *Wilson Bulletin*, Vol. 53, pp. 151-159, 1947.

Stewart, Paul, "Diving Schedules of the Common Loon," *Auk*, Vol. 84, pp. 122-123, 1967.

Woolfenden, Glen, "Selection for a Delayed Simultaneous Wing Molt in Loons," *Wilson Bulletin*, Vol. 79, pp. 416-420, 1967.

Disease/Chemical Contamination

Anderson, et.al. Editors, *Infectious and Parasitic Disease of Wild Birds*, Iowa State University Press, Ames, Iowa, 1976.

Brand, Christopher, et.al., "Waterbird Mortality from Botulism Type E in Lake Michigan: An Update," *Wilson Bulletin*, Vol. 95, pp. 269-275, 1983.

Graham, Frank, "Mystery at Dog Island," *Audubon*, pp. 30-34, March, 1984.

Farner, Donald and King, James, Editors, *Avian Biology, Vol. II*, Academic Press, New York, 1972.

Frank, R., et.al., "Residues of Organochlorine Insecticides, Industrial Chemicals and Mercury in Eggs and in Tissues Taken from Healthy and Emaciated Loons, Ontario, Canada, 1968-1980," *Archives of Environmental Contamination and Toxicology*, Vol. 12, pp. 641-645, 1983.

Lange, Robert and Stroud, Richard, "Information Summary of Common Loon Die-Off, Winter and Spring of 1983," U.S. Department of Interior, National Wildlife Health Laboratory, Madison, Wisconsin, 1983.

Locke, L. N., et.al., "Lead Poisoning in Common Loons," *Avian Diseases*, Vol. 26, No. 2, 1981.

Sutcliffe, Scott, "Pesticide Levels and Shell Thicknesses of Common Loon Eggs in New Hampshire," *Wilson Bulletin*, Vol. 90, pp. 637-640, 1978.

Native American Culture

Bierhorst, John, *Songs of the Chippewa*, Farar, Straus and Giroux, New York, 1974.

Clark, Ella E., *Indian Legends of the Pacific Northwest*, University of California Press, Berkeley, 1953.

Garfield, Viola and Forrest, Lin, *The Wolf and Raven: Totem Poles of Southeastern Alaska*, University of Washington Press, 1948.

Garber, Clark, *Stories and Legends of the Bering Strait Eskimos*, The Christopher Publishing House, Boston, 1940.

Gubser, Nicholas J., *Nunamiut Eskimos: Hunters of the Caribou*, Yale University Press, New Haven, 1965.

Hantzsch, Bernhard, *My Life Among the Eskimos*, Edited by L. H. Neatby, University of Saskatchewan, 1977.

Harper, Frances, *Caribou Eskimos of the Upper Kazan River*, University of Kansas, Lawrence, 1964.

Warner, William, *History of Ojibway Nation*, Ross and Haines, Inc., Minneapolis, 1974.

General Interest

Austin, Oliver, *Birds of the World*, Paul Hamlyn Ltd., London, 1961.

Bent, Arthur C., *Life Histories of North American Diving Birds*, Dover Publications, New York, 1919.

Chapman, Frank M., *Handbook of Birds in Eastern North America*, Dover Publications, New York, 1939.

Forbush, Edward H., *Natural History of Birds of Eastern and Central North America*, Houghton & Mifflin Co., Boston, 1939.

Godfrey, William E., *Birds of Canada*, National Museum of Canada Bulletin 203, Ottawa, 1966.

Palmer, Ralph S., *Handbook of North American Birds, Vol. I*, Yale University Press, New Haven, Connecticut, 1962.

Pearson, Gilbert T., *Birds of America*, Doubleday & Co., New York, 1917.

Peterson, Rogert T., *The Bird Watcher's Anthology*, Harcourt, Brace & Co., New York, 1957.

Storer, Robert, "The Fossil Loon, Colymboides Minutes," *The Condor*, Vol. 58, pp. 413-426, 1956.

INDEX

PHOTO BY LYNN ROGERS

COLOPHON

Designed by Phill Thill, Madison, Wisconsin

Typeset in Palatino with Palatino Italics by
Impressions, Inc., Madison, Wisconsin

Color separations and printing by Bruce Offset Company,
Elk Grove Village, Illinois

The text paper, Consolidated's Centura Dull, supplied by
Leslie Paper, Milwaukee, Wisconsin

Bound by Nicholstone Book Bindery,
Nashville, Tennessee

Published by Paper Birch Press, Inc.,
Pat Klein, Editor-in-Chief

PHOTO BY R. C. BURKE